SCIENCE FICTION
BEFORE 1900

IMAGINATION
DISCOVERS TECHNOLOGY

STUDIES IN LITERARY THEMES AND GENRES

Ronald Gottesman, Editor
University of Southern California

SCIENCE FICTION
BEFORE 1900

IMAGINATION
DISCOVERS TECHNOLOGY

Paul K. Alkon

Twayne Publishers
New York

Maxwell Macmillan Canada
Toronto

Maxwell Macmillan International
New York   Oxford   Singapore   Sydney

All illustrations are taken from the Eaton Collection copy of Albert Robida, *Le Vingtième Siècle* (Paris: Montgredien, 1892), and are reproduced with permission from the Eaton Collection at the University of California in Riverside.

Studies in Literary Themes and Genres No. 3

Twayne Publishers
Macmillan Publishing Company
866 Third Avenue
New York, New York 10022

Maxwell Macmillan Canada, Inc.
1200 Eglinton Avenue East
Suite 200
Don Mills, Ontario M3C 3N1

Library of Congress Cataloging-in-Publication Data

Alkon, Paul K. (Paul Kent)
   Science fiction before 1900: imagination discovers technology/Paul K. Alkon.
      p.   cm.—(Studies in literary themes and genres; no. 3)
   Includes bibligraphical references (p.) and index.
   ISBN 0-8057-0952-5
   1. Science fiction—History and criticism. 2. Fantastic fiction—History and criticism. 3. Science fiction—Bibliography. 4. Fantastic fiction—Bibliography. I. Title. II. Series.
PN3433.5.A45   1994   93-34821
809.3'876—dc20   CIP

The paper used in this publication meets the minimum requirements of American National Standard for Information Sciences—Permanence of Paper for Printed Library Materials. ANSI Z3948-1984. ⊚ ™

10 9 8 7 6 5 4 3 2   (hc)

Printed in the United States of America

For Pascal Ducommun

Who knows what the Utopian edition
of this book should contain

General Editor's Statement

Genre studies have been a central concern of Anglo-American and European literary theory for at least the past quarter century, and the academic interest has been reflected, for example, in new college courses in slave narratives, autobiography, biography, nature writing, and the literature of travel as well as in the rapid expansion of genre theory itself. Genre has also become an indispensable term for trade publishers and the vast readership they serve. Indeed, few general bookstores do not have sections devoted to science fiction, romance, and mystery fiction. Still, genre is among the slipperiest of literary terms, as any examination of genre theories and their histories will suggest.

In conceiving this series we have tried, on the one hand, to avoid the comically pedantic spirit that informs Polonius' recitation of kinds of drama and, on the other hand, the equally unhelpful insistence that every literary production is a unique expression that must not be forced into any system of classification. We have instead developed our list of genres, which range from ancient comedy to the Western, with the conviction that by common consent kinds of literature do exist—not as fixed categories but as fluid ones that change over time as the result of complex interplay of authors, audiences, and literary and cultural institutions. As individual titles in the series demonstrate, the idea of genre offers us provocative ways to study both the continuities and adaptability of literature as a familiar and inexhaustible source of human imagination.

Recognition of the fluid boundaries both within and among genres will provide, we believe, a useful array of perspectives from which to study literature's complex development. Genres, as traditional but open ways of understanding the world, contribute to our capacity to respond to narrative and expressive forms and offer means to discern moral significances embodied in these forms. Genres, in short, serve ethical as well as aesthetic purposes, and the volumes in this series attempt to demonstrate how this double benefit has been achieved as these genres have been transformed over the years. Each title in the series should be measured against this large ambition.

Ron Gottesman

Contents

Contents

Preface

Every fan of science fiction remembers with pleasure Arthur C. Clarke's classic 1953 short story "The Nine Billion Names of God." But I believe there would be few happy memories of an introduction to science fiction's early days that read like a catalog of the nine billion works before 1900 with some claim as precursors or exemplars of the genre. Of course there were not quite that many. There are, however, enough serious claimants so that to mention, let alone discuss, them all or even those most widely read in their time would create an impression of astronomical magnitude more bewildering than enlightening. I intend this book, therefore, to provide soundings rather than a survey. Those who know, or think they know, the history of science fiction will have the satisfaction of deploring my omission of many favorite and doubtless relevant texts that are among what I consider the "nine billion."

The very plenitude of works from which historians must choose and over whose claims they quarrel is a measure of science fiction's impressive scope and vitality. No recently crystallized genre touches on so many urgent human concerns and draws more widely on the resources of previous literature. No form better illustrates the dictum that genres serve ethical as well as aesthetic purposes. Science fiction excels at articulating the new possibilities for good and evil that shape our destinies in an age when science has accelerated the proliferation of technologies once beyond even the reach of fantasy. My selection has been governed by a conviction that the best science fiction has more often than not given powerful imaginative shape to those characteristically modern fears and hopes generated by the creative as well as the destructive potentials of advanced technology.

I use "technology" in its widest sense to mean applied science. Although technological change with drastic social consequences has been the most general impetus toward development of science fiction, as well as its master theme, this genre also owes much to the aesthetic impulse to vary literary forms, an impulse created by the dynamics of literature itself. Each successful work poses the challenge of imitating it with enough variations to achieve originality, thereby incorporating it into successor types and perhaps eventually supplanting it altogether. This game has always had its own attractions irrespective of the social contexts in which it is played or the ideas expressed: *Homo technicus* is also *Homo ludens*. My selection of texts for discussion has also been governed by the conviction that science fiction at its best is a distinctly self-conscious and self-referential genre that invites readers to appreciate the clever ways in which texts may allude to one another, to themselves, and to the act of reading.

In keeping with the wise editorial policy of Twayne's Studies in Literary Themes and Genres, I have concentrated on a few key works that mark the most significant phases in the early evolution of science fiction: Mary Shelley's *Frankenstein* (1818); Jules Verne's *Twenty Thousand Leagues Under the Sea* (1870); Albert Robida's *Le Vingtième siècle* (1883); Villiers de L'Isle-Adam's *Tomorrow's Eve* (1886); Edward Bellamy's *Looking Backward* (1888); Mark Twain's *A Connecticut Yankee in King Arthur's Court* (1889); and H. G. Wells's *The Time Machine* (1895) and *The War of the Worlds* (1898). By way of context and by way too of further orientation I also include shorter consideration of other works and related developments outside literature. To understand rightly what and how these key texts contribute to science fiction is to appreciate its advent as a distinct genre. My discussion even of these milestones is not designed to be exhaustive, however, but rather to provide orientation—and, I hope, stimulation—allowing my readers to acquaint or reacquaint themselves with these archetypes and with relevant criticism of them as a way of embarking on the right path to their own close encounter with the origins of science fiction. I have tried to provide a first, not the last, word. Ideally, this book will work something like one of Stanley Fish's self-consuming artifacts: after perusing its pages readers should go on to experience for themselves all the primary texts mentioned to discover riches only hinted at here, proceeding next to other works on the recommended list and finally to the secondary sources found in my Notes and References and my Bibliographic Essay. Whoever goes this full route will have received full benefit from *Science Fiction Before 1900*.

After discussing in chapter 1 science fiction's aesthetics to show what is at stake in defining this protean genre, along with some attention to its social context, I proceed to chapters on England, France, and America. This arrangement somewhat blurs chronological relationships, but these may easily be sorted out in prospect or retrospect by consulting the Chronology. I wish to stress that science fiction has from its outset been an international phenomenon transcending political boundaries while nevertheless taking on distinctive features that reflect different national preoccupations. English literature has been especially abundant in providing techniques for achieving what is described in *Frankenstein* as new viewpoints to the imagination. In treating France under the rubric "technophilia" and America under "technophobia" I am, as throughout this book, less concerned with simple head counting (which would have reversed these rubrics) than with identifying significant features of the best and therefore most important works. Hence my invitation to consider Mark Twain's too often neglected or underrated invention of time travel in a work expressing profound doubts about how technology shapes human history. Hence too my invitation to consider the ways in which Jules Verne, Villiers de L'Isle-Adam, and Albert Robida express their fascination with technology. These French authors are too little known outside their homeland, which has also received insufficient credit for taking the lead in authorship of tales set in future time. Verne is famous at least by name among Anglophone readers, though in fact seldom read, mostly known for the wrong reasons, and still underrated even among historians of science fiction, thanks to wretched English translations that were until recently the only ones available for his major works. I hope this book will help make Verne and his compatriots more properly appreciated and more frequently read.

I stop at the nineteenth century's close with some uneasiness at perhaps perpetuating neglect of the interesting interval between Verne's death in 1905 and Hugo Gernsback's inauguration of the *Amazing Stories* pulp magazine in 1926, which is often but not altogether accurately taken as the genre's modern starting point. To understand the achievement of twentieth-century science fiction, it is necessary to see how remarkably well its foundations had been established by 1900. I have fewer qualms about concentrating on those sturdy foundations when I recollect that Twayne's forthcoming volume on science fiction after 1900 will be from the expert hand of Brooks Landon, to whose pages I refer readers for a companion to my tale.

A few paragraphs in chapter 1 are adapted with the kind permission of the University of Delaware Press from my essay *"Gulliver* and the Origins of Science Fiction" in *The Genres of Gulliver's Travels*, ed. Frederik N. Smith (Newark: University of Delaware Press, 1990). Several paragraphs in chapters 2 and 3 are adapted with permission of the University of Georgia Press from my *Origins of Futuristic Fiction* (Athens: University of Georgia Press, 1987). I am grateful to Frederik Smith for insisting that I think about Swift and science fiction. I thank Karen Orchard for approving my truancy from Georgia. George Slusser of the University of California at Riverside has, as always, been a stimulating guide to the indispensable resources of the Eaton Collection. Michael A. Cropper, Librarian of the Los Angeles Maritime Museum, has kept my discussion of Verne from going aground on the reefs of ignorance. The OVDS ship *Nordnorge* took me safely past the Maelstrom to the Lofoten Islands with a good deal more comfort and less trouble than Professor Aronnax and Captain Nemo experienced off those fascinating shores. Dr. Laura E. Fox maintains my sight but cannot be blamed for my conclusions about what I see. Sylvia K. Miller has provided helpful advice with saintly patience. Timothy J. DeWerff expertly supervised this book's final countdown. Ronald Gottesman's exemplary collegiality has been as inspiring as his refreshing fidelity to the idea that genres are important because imaginative literature matters. In my voyage on this sea of words, as in other voyages, Ellen has been my ideal shipmate.

Chronology

1516   Sir Thomas More's *Utopia*.

1590   Compound microscope is invented by Zacharias Janssen.

1609   Galileo makes his first telescope.

1634   Johannes Kepler's *Somnium* (*The Dream*).

1638   Francis Godwin's *The Man in the Moon; or, A Discourse of a Voyage Thither by Domingo Gonsales*.

1657   Cyrano de Bergerac's *Histoire comique des états et empires de la lune* (*Comic History of the States and Empires of the Moon*).

1659   Jacques Guttin's *Epigone, histoire du siècle futur* (Epigone, a story of the future century).

1662   Cyrano de Bergerac's *Histoire comique des états et empires du soleil* (*Comic History of the States and Empires of the Sun*).

1719   Daniel Defoe's *Robinson Crusoe*.

1722   Daniel Defoe's *A Journal of the Plague Year*.

1726   Jonathan Swift's *Gulliver's Travels*.

1752   Voltaire's *Micromégas*.

1769   James Watt builds a practical steam engine.

1771   Louis-Sébastien Mercier's *L'An 2440* (The year 2440).

1783   Pilâtre de Rozier makes first human flight, in a hot-air balloon invented by Jacques and Joseph Montgolfier.

1797   Mary Wollstonecraft Shelley is born.

1798   Thomas Malthus's *An Essay on the Principle of Population.*

1801   Robert Fulton builds a submarine, named *Nautilus,* for France.

1802   Nicolas-Edme Restif de la Bretonne's *Les Posthumes* (The posthumous).

1804   First steam locomotive.

1805   Jean-Baptiste Xavier Cousin de Grainville's *Le Dernier homme* (*The Last Man*).

1809   Edgar Allan Poe is born.

1818   Mary Shelley's *Frankenstein; or, The Modern Prometheus.*

1825   The Stockton and Darlington, in England, is the first regularly operated steam railroad.

1826   Mary Shelley's *The Last Man.*

1827   Jane Webb's *The Mummy: A Tale of the Twenty-Second Century.*

1828   Jules Verne is born.

1831   Mary Shelley's revised edition of *Frankenstein.*

1834   Félix Bodin's *Le Roman de l'avenir* (The novel of the future).

1835   Edgar Allan Poe's "The Unparalleled Adventure of One Hans Pfaall." Mark Twain [Samuel Langhorne Clemens] is born.

1836   Louis-Napoléon Geoffroy-Château's *Napoléon et la conquête du monde* (Napoleon and the conquest of the world).

1838   Villiers de l'Isle Adam is born. The British
        steamship *Sirius* makes the first transatlantic
        crossing under continuous steam power.

1844   Edgar Allan Poe's "The Balloon Hoax" and
        "Mesmeric Revelation."

1846   Emile Souvestre's *Le Monde tel qu'il sera* (The
        world as it will be).

1848   Albert Robida is born.

1849   Edgar Allan Poe's "Mellonta Tauta"; Poe dies.

1850   Edward Bellamy is born.

1851   Mary Shelley dies.

1854   Charlemagne-Ischir Defontenay's *Star ou psi de
        Cassiopée* (*Star: Psi Cassiopeia*).

1859   Charles Darwin's *On the Origin of Species by
        Means of Natural Selection*.

1861   Transcontinental telegraph is established in
        North America.

1863   Jules Verne's *Cinq Semaines en ballon* (*Five Weeks
        in a Balloon*).

1865   Jules Verne's *De la Terre à la lune* (*From the Earth
        to the Moon*).

1866   H. G. Wells is born. Transatlantic telegraph is
        established.

1870   *Vingt mille lieues sous les mers* (*Twenty Thousand
        Leagues Under the Sea*): Jules Verne's *Autour de la
        lune* (*Around the Moon*).

1871   Sir George T. Chesney's *The Battle of Dorking*.

1872   Samuel Butler's *Erewhon; or, Over the Range*.

1873   *Le Tour du monde en quatre-vingts jours* (*Around the
        World in Eighty Days*).

1874–1875   Jules Verne's *L'Ile mystérieuse* (*The Mysterious
        Island*).

1876   Alexander Graham Bell invents the telephone.

1877   Jules Verne's *Hector Servadac*. Thomas A. Edison
        invents the first practical phonograph.

1879 Jules Verne's *Les Cinq Cents Millions de la Bégum* (*The Bégum's Fortune*). Thomas A. Edison invents the electric light with carbon filament.

1883 Albert Robida's *Le Vingtième siècle* (The twentieth century); *La Vie électrique* (The electric life).

1884 Edwin A. Abbott's *Flatland: A Romance of Many Dimensions*.

1886 Robert Louis Stevenson's *The Strange Case of Dr. Jekyll and Mr. Hyde*. Jules Verne's *Robur le conquérant* (*The Clipper of the Clouds*). Villiers de l'Isle-Adam's *L'Eve future* (*Tomorrow's Eve*).

1887 Albert Robida's *La Guerre au vingtième siècle* (War in the twentieth century). J. H. Rosny Aîné's [Joseph-Henri Honoré Boëx] "Les Xipéhuz" (*The Xipehuz*). Sir Henry Rider Haggard's *She*.

1888 Edward Bellamy's *Looking Backward: 2000–1887*.

1889 Mark Twain's *A Connecticut Yankee in King Arthur's Court*. Jules Verne's *Sans dessus dessous* (*The Purchase of the North Pole*). Villiers de l'Isle-Adam dies.

1891 William Morris's *News from Nowhere*.

1893 Nicolas Camille Flammarion's *La Fin du monde* (*Omega: The Last Days of the World*). George Griffith's *The Angel of the Revolution*.

1895 H. G. Wells's *The Time Machine; The Stolen Bacillus and Other Incidents*.

1896 H. G. Wells's *The Island of Doctor Moreau*.

1897 Kurd Lasswitz's *Auf zwei Planeten* (*Two Planets*). H. G. Wells's *The Invisible Man*.

1898 Edward Bellamy dies. Garrett Putnam Serviss's *Edison's Conquest of Mars*. H. G. Wells's *The War of the Worlds*.

1899 H. G. Wells's *When the Sleeper Wakes: A Story of Years to Come; Tales of Space and Time*.

1900 First U.S. Navy submarine, the *Holland*, is commissioned.

1901   H. G. Wells's *The First Men in the Moon*.

1903   Wilbur and Orville Wright's biplane makes first flight, at Kitty Hawk, North Carolina.

1904   H. G. Wells's *The Food of the Gods, and How It Came to Earth*.

1905   Jules Verne dies. H. G. Wells's *A Modern Utopia*.

1906   H. G. Wells's *In the Days of the Comet*.

1907   Jack London's *The Iron Heel*.

1908   H. G. Wells's *The War in the Air*.

1909   E[dward] M[organ] Forster's "The Machine Stops."

1910   Mark Twain dies.

1911   H. G. Wells's *The Country of the Blind and Other Stories*.

1912   Sir Arthur Conan Doyle's *The Lost World*.

1914   H. G. Wells's *The World Set Free*.

1915   Charlotte Perkins Gilman's *Herland*.

1917   Edgar Rice Burroughs's *A Princess of Mars*.

1919   In "A Method of Reaching Extreme Altitudes," published by the Smithsonian Institution, Robert H. Goddard proposes sending a rocket to the moon.

1926   Albert Robida dies. Robert H. Goddard builds the first liquid-fuel rocket.

1945   United States uses atomic bombs in war against Japan.

1946   H. G. Wells dies.

1969   United States spaceship commanded by Neil A. Armstrong lands on the moon.

1

A Short History of the Future

Everything must have a beginning, to speak in Sanchean phrase;
and that beginning must be linked to something that went before.
The Hindus give the world an elephant to support it, but they
make the elephant stand upon a tortoise.

Mary Shelley, "Author's Introduction"
to the 1831 edition of *Frankenstein*

Definitions and Aesthetics of Science Fiction

Science fiction starts with Mary Shelley's *Frankenstein*. Its first
critic was Percy Shelley. For his wife he wrote a preface that (as
she explains in her 1831 introduction) was printed in the 1818
edition as though it were by her. If this ventriloquism betrays
some hesitancy in launching a new kind of tale, *Frankenstein*
itself displays such confident mastery that for almost two centuries it has rewarded the attention of readers and inspired writers in a genre largely devoted to variations on its theme of the
uses and abuses of science. *Frankenstein*'s 1818 preface distinguishes between its scientific plot and the more familiar action of
Gothic fiction: "I have not considered myself as merely weaving

a series of supernatural terrors. The event on which the interest of the story depends is exempt from the disadvantages of a mere tale of spectres or enchantment."[1] There is no mistaking the dismissive tone of these references to "mere" stories of ghosts or magic. By printing this statement as her own, Mary Shelley endorsed what Percy Shelley understood: that *Frankenstein*'s claim to originality is its rejection of the supernatural. Science fiction can only exist when it is possible to distinguish in this way between natural and supernatural as realms that very differently create "the interest of the story."

Paradoxically, however, neither *Frankenstein*'s 1818 preface nor its 1831 introduction by Mary Shelley renounces the goal of inducing "terrors." Quite the contrary. Terror remains a desirable effect. It is only supernatural terrors that are to be avoided. Readers are to be frightened by natural means involving science. In suggesting that fear can be achieved by a new kind of plot, *Frankenstein*'s preface and introduction stress both its claim to novelty and its affiliation to accepted Gothic forms subsumed under the label "ghost story." Although this identifies precursors, the affiliation is more than a matter of ancestry.

The affinities of science fiction and Gothic literature also reveal a common quest for those varieties of pleasing terror induced by awe-inspiring events or settings that Edmund Burke and other eighteenth-century critics called the sublime. A looming problem for writers in the nineteenth century was how to achieve sublimity without recourse to the supernatural. In 1819 John Keats famously complained in *Lamia* that science was emptying the haunted air. The supernatural marvels that had been a staple of epic and lesser forms from Homeric times would no longer do as the best sources of sublimity. Although ghost stories and related Gothic fantasies were to prove surprisingly viable right through the twentieth century, perhaps because they offer respite from the omnipresence of technology, writers sought new forms that could better accommodate the impact of science. Epics were displaced by realistic novels of quotidian life. By 1800 even William Wordsworth could imagine a time when "the remotest discoveries of the Chemist, the Botanist, or Mineralogist, will be as proper objects of the Poet's art as any upon which it can be employed."[2] Only sixteen years after *Frankenstein*, Félix Bodin argued for the importance of futuristic fiction, works set in future time, for which he invented the term *littérature futuriste* in his brilliantly prophetic 1834 novel-cum-manifesto, *Le Roman de l'avenir* (The novel of the future).

Bodin eloquently urges writers to turn away from the past and present, and also from boring utopias, to find plots combining interesting novelistic action with realistic visions of future social and technological possibilities such as aerial warfare and undersea voyages. He predicts that such works will become the epics of the future by finding new sources of the marvelous that are altogether credible, unlike the gods and other supernatural marvels in classical epics. Thus futuristic fiction alone, Bodin suggests, can appeal to our hunger for the marvelous while also remaining within the bounds of verisimilitude in a scientific age, thereby providing an artistically satisfying vehicle for rational speculation.[3] He links the aesthetic issue of imaginative appeal with the moral question of how people may be aroused from indifference to their own futures. Bodin's 1834 manifesto articulating a poetics of futuristic fiction did more than anticipate techniques that have become one hallmark of science fiction. Underlying his advocacy of the future as a significant new arena for human imagination is an interest as keen as Mary Shelley's in finding new sources of the marvelous that will allow literature to retain its emotional power without turning away from science.

Science fiction ever since has been concerned as often to elicit strong emotional responses as to maintain a rational basis for its plots. Far from being mutually exclusive, the two aims can reinforce each other, as they do in *Frankenstein* and in Mary Shelley's own futuristic novel published in 1826, *The Last Man*, which describes a terrifying twenty-first-century plague that destroys the human race. The balance may shift along a spectrum from emphasis on ideas, technology, or alien encounters to emphasis on their emotional consequences. At the rational end of the spectrum are novels like Hal Clement's classic *Mission of Gravity* (1954), which avoids depicting or eliciting emotion in favor of concentrating on the technical problems of human-alien relationships on a high-gravity planet with life forms based on a chemistry different from our own and evolving culturally toward a society that can use scientific method. Works like Ridley Scott's *Blade Runner* (1982) and Stanisław Lem's *Solaris* (1961) depict and surely aim to arouse strong emotions, among them fear, while also providing a scientific plot framework that raises philosophical issues of creation and human identity very much in the tradition of *Frankenstein* (1818). Films like the *Aliens* trilogy (1979, 1986, 1992) retain a scientific framework of futuristic space travel that keeps them within the boundaries of science fiction while tipping the balance toward effects of Gothic terror: instead of evil spirits, malignant aliens must be exorcised. With so many works at this end of the spectrum it is no wonder that some critics invoke *Frankenstein* mainly for the procrustean purpose of identifying all science fiction as little more than a variant of the Gothic mode with spaceships and horrifying aliens substituted for the creepy old haunted castles favored by Horace Walpole, Anne Radcliffe, and their successors to and beyond Stephen King in the line of pure Gothic.

But Mary Shelley achieved far more than a variation on well-known themes. She and Percy Shelley were right to deny so emphatically any equation of her novel and the "mere" ghost stories that served as one but only one inspiration for it. *Frankenstein*'s preface and introduction provide accounts of that famous rainy summer of 1816 near Geneva when she, Percy Shelley, John Polidori, and Lord Byron amused themselves by reading ghost stories and then accepted Byron's challenge to try their own hands at this form. Of the four who thus started in emulation of supernatural tales, only Mary Shelley finished a narrative, although she deviated from her literary models because science too caught her imagination. Reminiscing about that summer in the 1831 introduction, she tells of trying to imagine "a story to rival those which had excited us to this task. One which would speak to the mysterious fears of our nature and awaken thrilling horror—one to make the reader dread to look round, to curdle the blood, and quicken the beatings of the heart" (*Frankenstein*, ix). She *also* recounts listening to a conversation about Erasmus Darwin's biological experiments, about galvanism, and about possible ways of creating life by reanimating a corpse or else manufacturing "component parts of a creature" that might somehow be endowed with vitality. Not surprisingly, there followed a vivid nightmare of just such a creature contemplated by its "horror-stricken" creator. From this dream Mary Shelley says she woke "in terror" with "a thrill of fear" that soon gave way to realization that here at last was the starting point for

a tale that could frighten others just as she herself was frightened: "I began that day with the words [now opening chapter 5
of *Frankenstein*] It was on a dreary night of November,' making
only a transcript of the grim terrors of my waking dream"
(*Frankenstein*, xi). For Mary Shelley it is the dream of science, not
the sleep of reason, that produces monsters. The imaginative
genesis of *Frankenstein*, as of so much science fiction, is thus in
the transition from contemplation of scientific possibilities to
writing a story that preserves something like the effects of a disturbing dream, while grounding those effects in plots that do not
depend on supernatural events.

Neither, however, do such plots necessarily command belief
even as possibilities, much less as probabilities. *Frankenstein*'s
1818 preface confronts the inescapable illogic often necessary to
justify science fiction's solution (or evasion) of the difficult problem of achieving adequate verisimilitude. Percy Shelley starts by
insisting that the artificial creation of life central to *Frankenstein* is
not impossible according to "Dr. Darwin and some of the physio-
logical writers of Germany." Here is the fundamental gambit of
all science fiction: appeal to the speculations of real scientists as
an impeccable source of what follows in the fictional narrative.
The very next sentence, however, warns readers not to suppose
that the author gives "the remotest degree of serious faith to
such an imagination." What saves this startling about-face from
simply undermining the tale altogether is the ensuing observation that a plot based on Victor Frankenstein's animation of the
monster "however impossible as a physical fact, affords a point
of view to the imagination for the delineating of human passions
more comprehensive and commanding than any which the ordinary relations of existing events can yield" (*Frankenstein*, xiii).
Percy Shelley realized that the key issue for Mary Shelley's new
kind of tale is not whether its scientific premise is believable—it
was not—but whether a story based on such a premise can
achieve a valuable "point of view to the imagination." The role of
science in *Frankenstein*, as in so much subsequent science fiction,
is not so much to consider scientific realities as to afford a unique
vantage point for contemplation of the human condition.

We may now accept this slippery proposition more easily
thanks to our familiarity with tales of time travel, faster-than-
light spaceships, antigravity devices, and similar impossibilities

that have become established science fiction conventions. The genre's grand paradox, clearly articulated in the preface to *Frankenstein*, is that while a scientific premise is important, belief in its possibility is not. The science in science fiction may but does not have to be its main concern or even its claim to verisimilitude. Allusion to science more often, as in *Frankenstein*, serves a crucial enabling role: it allows for perspectives not otherwise attainable. *This* is the great leap away from Gothic.

Why science can allow perspectives not duplicated by tales of the supernatural based on elves, ghosts, magic, or the like, is a question that I shall for the moment defer as resolutely as Percy Shelley avoids it in the preface to *Frankenstein*. Here I will only remark that this question has become more insistent in the latter part of the twentieth century as science fiction once more converges on the forms of supernatural tale from which Mary Shelley dissociated it. The differences between science fiction and fantasy, though clear at either extreme, are becoming increasingly blurred at the boundaries. This recombining of genres is partly a consequence of post-Hiroshima disillusionment with the products of science and rationalism. As we retreat from Enlightenment certainties, our genres too lose their clarity. A more fundamental cause is twentieth-century acceleration of scientific innovation, which validates Arthur Clarke's dictum that to outsiders—and with respect to real science most of us are outsiders—a sufficiently advanced technology would be indistinguishable from magic. This aphorism has in turn gained relevance from the blurring within late-twentieth-century science fiction of the boundaries between natural and supernatural, as, for example, in the voodoo and other godlike entities that haunt the cyberspace of William Gibson's *Neuromancer*, *Count Zero*, and *Mona Lisa Overdrive*.[4] What matters for the early history of science fiction is Mary Shelley's realization and Percy Shelley's endorsement of the notion, however paradoxical, that valuable new perspectives can be achieved by recourse to science even if it is incredible science.

One hundred and fifteen years after the publication of *Frankenstein* that notion was endorsed too by H. G. Wells reminiscing in a preface to the 1933 edition of his early scientific romances. After characterizing the tales of Jules Verne as dealing "almost always with actual possibilities of invention and discovery," Wells remarks that his own stories, unlike Verne's, "do not aim to project a serious possibility; they aim indeed only at the same amount of conviction as one gets in a good gripping dream."[5] Here again is the idea of striving for the vividness of a dream by means of an apparently scientific premise. *Frankenstein* is among the works that Wells retrospectively classifies in this preface as like his own. Jules Verne toward the end of his career was equally careful to distinguish his technique from that of H. G. Wells. Interviewed in 1903, two years before his death, Verne remarked of Wells, "We do not proceed in the same manner. It occurs to me that his stories do not repose on very scientific bases. No, there is no *rapport* between his work and mine. I make use of physics. He invents. I go to the moon in a cannon-ball, discharged from a cannon. Here there is no invention. He goes to Mars in an airship, which he constructs of a metal which does away with the law of gravitation. *Ca c'est très joli* . . . but show me this metal. Let him produce it."[6] Verne makes a valid distinction here despite his apparent confusion of Wells's *The First Men in the Moon* with a story about travel to Mars. Wells and Verne were right to disclaim identity of method although Verne, for reasons that I discuss in chapter 3, does himself less than justice in claiming for his stories no more than the virtues of scientific accuracy according to the science of his day. Nor, for that matter, did Wells do his attention to science full justice in the self-deprecatory mood of his preface to the 1933 edition of his youthful science fiction tales, although he was right to call them "romances" and distinguish them from Verne's oeuvre in the matter of scientific precision. Verne in his way, no less than Wells and Mary Shelley in theirs, uses science as a springboard to creation of powerful myths allowing novel points of view to the imagination.

Science fiction might indeed be defined as the narrative use of science to create myths allowing novel points of view to the imagination—adding, to be sure, the caveat that such a definition is normative rather than descriptive since not all science fiction succeeds in creating such myths, much less in creating myths so powerful as those established by the genre's masterpieces from *Frankenstein* through *Nineteen Eighty-Four* and beyond. But even thus qualified, this definition neither covers all works commonly termed science fiction nor does it suggest all the aesthetic considerations necessary for understanding as well as judging their artistry. Nor do any other definitions so far proposed.

The term *science fiction* was coined in an obscure 1851 text, William Wilson's *A Little Earnest Book upon a Great Old Subject*, and then forgotten. The phrase gained currency only after Hugo Gernsback reinvented it in 1929 to replace his less graceful neologism "scientifiction" as a description for the project of *Amazing Stories*, the magazine he founded in 1926. Its announced aim was to stimulate fiction that would continue what Gernsback saw as the tradition of Edgar Allan Poe, Jules Verne, and H. G. Wells. Gernsback's success in largely creating as well as naming the twentieth-century pulp realm of science fiction is legendary, as is the subsequent growth of that form outside its early confines. But there is still no consensus on how to define the genre despite—or more likely because of—its twentieth-century proliferation. One must live on some other planet to escape close encounters with avatars of science fiction widely recognized as such, definition or no definition.

From literature the genre has expanded into movies, television, comic strips, advertising, and other aspects of contemporary life. Common habits of thinking have become science fictional because the borderline between art and reality blurs as we confront a world that so often reminds us of science fiction. We contemplate its echoes in images of real space travel while sitting before our television screens watching shuttles take off and land or while turning over the old albums showing photographs of our astronauts visiting the moon. We try to cope with proliferation of high-tech weaponry that threatens to annihilate our planet while seeming to future-shocked sensibilities like an importation from films like *Star Wars*, after which some of the weapon systems are named. Warnings of ecological disasters ahead remind us of doomsday novels in the tradition of *The Last Man*. Upon finishing books like *Neuromancer* that teem with futuristic cyborgs, we may read a sober estimate that as of 1990 "about 10 percent of the U.S. population *are* cyborgs, including people who have electronic pacemakers, artificial joints, prosthetic limbs, and artificial skin."[7] We favor such architecture as the Los Angeles Bonaventure Hotel that can serve equally as an exterior setting of "New Chicago" for a recent television series called "Buck Rogers in the Twenty-Fifth Century" and as Fredric

Jameson's prime illustration of the postmodern space that we increasingly inhabit in the late twentieth century.[8] Vehicle names take us back and forth from the real world to science fiction as we contemplate warships named *Enterprise*, Star Trek's spaceship of that name, and the American space shuttle *Enterprise*. Less than a century after Jules Verne honored Robert Fulton's 1801 submersible *Nautilus* by giving its name in 1870 to Captain Nemo's submarine, the U.S. Navy paid splendid homage to Verne's *Twenty Thousand Leagues Under the Sea* as well as to Fulton's ship by naming our first nuclear-powered submarine the USS *Nautilus* in 1955. Conflation of present objects with science fiction's iconography of the future creates the sensation of life as science fiction. Such allusive interchanges reveal a twentieth-century mentality in which a broadly conceived notion of science fiction is among our fixed mental reference points. The polysemy of the term *science fiction*, reflected in the inability of critics to arrive at agreement on any one definition, is a measure of science fiction's complex significance for our times.

Inevitably, then, our view of science fiction's past is colored by awareness of its many present roles in and outside of literature. So are the competing definitions. Their disparity reflects the impossibility of neatly accounting for everything science fiction, in its widest sense, now does to shape our worldview. Their disparity also reflects difficulties in describing a genre that was hardly consolidated when its material transcended the written word. Without falling into the teleological fallacy of seeing everything in the past as leading only to ourselves and our preoccupations of the moment, any history of science fiction must consider not only the emergence of its prototypes as they were regarded by their authors and contemporaries, but also those reciprocal relationships by which later developments forever change our view of earlier works. *Frankenstein* exemplifies this process. Widening agreement that it is science fiction's beginning place reflects increasing awareness after 1945 that in it Mary Shelley embodied what now seems the central myth for an age wherein the unparalleled creativity of science threatens the world with unprecedented disasters. Victor Frankenstein's dangerous monster turning on its creator has become the twentieth century's archetypal emblem. When Hiroshima was destroyed, *Frankenstein* irrevocably became science fiction.

Of course in calling *Frankenstein* science fiction, as Mark Rose observes, "we are retroactively recomposing that text under the influence of a generic idea that did not come into being until well after it was written."[9] This procedure is common (though not always remarked) in the history of literary genres. Plato's *Republic*, for example, is seen as a forerunner of utopian forms because we regard it today in the light of all those speculative fictions closely or distantly modeled on Sir Thomas More's *Utopia* (1516). Such realignment depends on "conceiving genre as a social phenomenon, as a set of expectations rather than as something that resides within a text" (Rose, 5). Thus defined, genre is constituted by reading conventions that allow or compel attention to focus on a set of textual features which thereby acquire special prominence—and perhaps special consequences—for particular readers. A complicated text may offer several generic options that are not mutually exclusive. Accordingly it can play a role in the history of more than one genre, as *Frankenstein* certainly does no less than many other texts I discuss in this book, although I am concerned here only with their role as science fiction.

Among the most useful definitions of science fiction are those which take into account the new ways of reading it has fostered. Samuel Delany argues that science fiction is distinctive by virtue of the degree to which it focuses attention on disparities between our universe—of discourse no less than of daily life—and that evoked by a narrative: "with each sentence we have to ask what in the world of the tale would have to be different from our world for such a sentence to be uttered—and thus, as the sentences build up, we build up a world in specific dialogue, in a specific tension, with our present concept of the real."[10] This is a way of reading much encouraged by science fiction. But every form of fantasy, allegory, utopia, and satire, after all, is in some kind of dialogue with our notions of reality. To specify essential differences between these forms and science fiction—with which they may coexist in the same work—Darko Suvin has argued influentially for taking science fiction as the literature of cognitive estrangement.

By this, Suvin means literature that not only defamiliarizes aspects of the ordinary world that we inhabit, but that does so in ways inviting awareness (cognition) of the *principles* governing those features of life that we are invited to regard as unfamiliar—

as though we were, perhaps, alien anthropologists visiting this planet to study it, taking nothing for granted beforehand. Cognition is involved whenever the defamiliarized subject is understood on a more rational basis as a contingent phenomenon whose conditions, if known, may be subject to control or even alteration rather than simply unquestioning acceptance. Suvin's example, borrowed from Bertolt Brecht, is Galileo's ability to look at a swinging chandelier with sufficient detachment to see its movement as strange enough to require an explanation, which he then provided in stating the laws governing pendulum motion. Awareness of these laws, in turn, allows a measure of control over such motion and application of it to new purposes. Suvin concludes that science fiction is "a literary genre whose necessary and sufficient conditions are the presence and interaction of estrangement and cognition, and whose main formal device is an imaginative framework alternative to the author's empirical environment."[11]

By stressing cognition as a consequence *for readers* of narrative defamiliarization achieved via depiction of an alternative environment, Suvin's definition of science fiction distinguishes between it and such forms as myth, folk tale, and fantasy that neither so insistently call into question our sense of the world as it is nor by doing so invite readers to adopt a critical outlook with strong affinities to scientific method. As this definition implies, and as Mary Shelley clearly intuited in turning to science and not the supernatural as a basis for *Frankenstein*'s plot, it is invocation of a rational worldview implied by affinities with the scientific method that allows science fiction, even when based on incredible science, to serve purposes distinct from those of more traditional fantasy. The question that Percy Shelley avoided in *Frankenstein*'s 1818 preface and that I deferred is thus answered. This definition allows for continuities with related forms that may approach science fictional effects. It too is a normative rather than merely descriptive definition, since most science fiction fails to elicit radical new understanding of our own world. As in other genres, only the best work fully realizes the form's potentialities. The virtue of definitions like those proposed by Delany and Suvin is their emphasis on the interaction of readers and texts rather than on theme and technique as the primary elements of genre.

To focus on content, usually with emphasis on how prominently science (or what looks likes science or was once taken for
science) figures as a theme is to cast a very wide net that usually
retrieves more bits and pieces than whole works and that lumps
together very different specimens. The best of such definitions is
Pierre Versins's concept of science fiction as the novelistic literature of rational conjecture. This notion allowed Versins to under-
take a magnificent feat of book collection and bibliographical
organization that led first to his indispensable *Encyclopédie de
l'Utopie, des voyages extraordinaires, et de la science fiction*
(Encyclopedia of utopias, extraordinary voyages, and science fiction), then to establishment in 1976 of the Maison d'Ailleurs
(House of Elsewhere): a science fiction museum at Yverdon-les-
Bains, Switzerland, which now houses the original Versins collection of some twenty-five thousand volumes, adds to it, hosts
conferences, and provides researchers with Europe's most extensive library of early science fiction and related literature.
Whatever lacks an element of rational conjecture is ruled out of
this enterprise, which thus excludes most but not all outright
fantasy—depending on how rigorously one defines what is
rational. The chief virtue of this definition is inclusiveness, as
witness the size of the Versins collection and the corresponding
scope of his encyclopedia. Both are treasure troves for those concerned with various more narrowly defined genres, especially
utopias and imaginary voyages, that have contributed to the rise
of science fiction. But to accept every narrative with some element of rational conjecture as science fiction is to acknowledge
its larger cultural role while clouding awareness of its distinct literary identity and its ways of incorporating related forms. This
Versins understood very well. In the introduction to his
Encyclopédie he concedes that "novelistic rational conjecture is a
point of view on the universe, including mankind, and neither a
genre nor a form."[12] But to write a history of conjecture about the
universe, even if confined to novelistic conjecture, would be a
formidable task.

Greater attention to science fictional modes of reading rather
than textual themes results in sharper focus on distinctive generic features, more attention to the aesthetics of entire works, and
establishment of a manageable canon. A case in point is Jonathan
Swift's *Gulliver's Travels* (1726). Its affinities with science fiction

have long been acknowledged. But there is disagreement on the nature of those affinities. Some propose it as no more than an honorable ancestor, listed mainly to provide the family tree with an air of respectability. Others agree with Darko Suvin's suggestion that *Gulliver's Travels*, not *Frankenstein*, is science fiction's very archetype.

For those who define science fiction mainly in terms of how far scientific concepts explicitly enter its subject matter, Gulliver's voyages to Lilliput (the land of little people) and to Brobdingnag (the land of giants) are adventure-fantasy no matter how much they may have been inspired by invention of the microscope and telescope. Swift's consistently presented details of size relationships in the first two voyages merely foreshadow the techniques of science fiction in portraying alien environments with verisimilitude. Gulliver's third voyage is science fiction, but only while he is on the magnetically controlled Flying Island of Laputa, in Lagado at the Grand Academy with its mad scientists, and among the long-lived Struldbruggs. The fourth voyage with its account of the land of rational horses is a variety of utopia. In this view, *Gulliver's Travels* as a whole lacks generic unity but is no worse for that. Insofar as it is science fiction it is deplorable for the very cleverness of its attack on science, but no more deplorable than any other kind of antiscientific rhetoric. Swift gets credit—from Isaac Asimov, among others—for being the first English writer of true science fiction but is found reprehensible for his hostility to science and his lack of faith in the idea of progress.[13] Partly on account of taking these negative attitudes as a rhetorical stance, the third voyage, despite its virtues as pioneering science fiction, seems the weakest. Swift remains the foremost English satirist, but *Gulliver's Travels* is relegated to the remote past of science fiction.

For those who define science fiction in terms of reader response, Swift is our contemporary. The eighteenth century is in active dialogue with the twentieth century. In *Gulliver's Travels*, Suvin eloquently insists, "Swift created the great model for all subsequent SF. It is a wise interweaving of utopias taking on anti-utopian functions and anti-utopias as allies of utopianism: of satire using scientific language and technological extrapolation as a grotesque; of adventures in SF countries, artificial satellites and aliens, immortals and monsters, all signifying

England and the gentle reader. All the later protagonists of SF, gradually piecing together their strange locales, are sons of Gulliver, and all their more or less cognitive adventures the continuation of his *Travels*" (Suvin, 113). In this view *Gulliver's Travels* becomes a unified work with all of its components— imaginary voyage, utopia, anti-utopia, fantasy, and satire—subordinated as parts of a coherent whole because amid their various purposes they all help sustain cognitive estrangement. Other effects may predominate locally. But *Gulliver's Travels* propels readers through varying degrees of strangeness and corresponding arousal of cognitive estrangement to an appropriate climax (not simply a conundrum for critics) in the fourth part.

Gulliver's last voyage, rather than the third voyage, becomes the most powerful science fiction in *Gulliver's Travels* because, of all the creatures Gulliver encounters, the Houyhnhnms are the most genuinely alien—the most shockingly different. Neither in their shape, their mentality, nor their social forms do they recall humans, that is to say, *our* world—as do the Lilliputians, the Brobdingnagians, and even the mad scientists of Laputa and Lagado. The Houyhnhnms are truly other. Their appearance, their well-ordered society, their honesty, and above all their refusal to love or hate as we do drives Gulliver mad—and too often drives critics in the same direction by their endless dispute over Swift's intentions. When *Gulliver's Travels* is taken as science fiction there is no need to enter that hopeless debate. Rather than asking the unanswerable question of whether Swift intended readers to accept the Houyhnhnms as Gulliver does for a model in all things, we may take the evident difficulty of doing so—we can hardly become talking horses devoid of emotion—as a measure of Swift's success in making readers look at humanity from a radically estranged perspective. For any thinking person that perspective in turn is an invitation to assess the springs of human behavior instead of just taking note of the myriad forms of human folly satirized en route to Gulliver's final lodging in the stable where he prefers to live among his horses rather than with his wife and family. Heightened awareness by contrast with the Houyhnhnms of what we are, rather than identification of any explicit utopian proposal from Swift of what to do about our shortcomings, can be taken as a satisfactory outcome of reading *Gulliver's Travels*.

While there have been other critical routes to a similar conclusion, looking back to see *Gulliver's Travels* as a pioneer in the literature of cognitive estrangement allows specification not merely of its satiric targets but of its continuing vitality as a prototype for science fiction that invites consideration of why as well as how human society so often goes wrong. But this is also true of *Frankenstein* despite its narrower range of topics. Whatever the starting point of science fiction, social criticism has been a prominent feature of the genre. A key difference between *Gulliver's Travels* and *Frankenstein* is the centrality—for readers as well as within the plot—of Mary Shelley's allusion to science, symbolized by Victor Frankenstein's creation of artificial life. Although it enriches our understanding of relationships between the eighteenth and twentieth centuries to appropriate *Gulliver's Travels* for science fiction thanks to its alien encounters that induce an estranged reconsideration of ourselves, recent history has even more fully underscored the significance and mythic force of *Frankenstein*'s focus on science.

Contexts and Precursors

The scientific experiments that led to Mary Shelley's creative nightmare, and thence to science fiction, were among new developments that were altering the conditions of human life more drastically, and above all more rapidly, than ever before. A centenarian born in the year of *Frankenstein*'s publication to a world of sailboats, balloons, horse-drawn carriages, slow experimental locomotives and steamships, semaphore signals, stage shows, and mesmerism would have departed a planet amused by cinema, treated for its worries by psychoanalysis, divided by a world war of unprecedented ferocity, and linked by an intricate network of fast steamships, railroads, airplanes, telephones, telegraphs, transatlantic cables, and radios. When H. G. Wells took stock and tried to forecast twentieth-century developments in his 1901 opus *Anticipations of the Reaction of Mechanical and Scientific Progress upon Human Life and Thought*, he concluded that the most conspicuous feature of all history prior to the nineteenth century was the very slow pace of change: "Consider, for example, how entirely in sympathy was the close of the eigh-

teenth century with the epoch of Horace, and how closely equivalent were the various social aspects of the two periods."[14]
Although Wells exaggerates similarities persisting over some two
thousand years, it is nevertheless revealing that a founder of science fiction should so stress this particular point. Nor was he
wrong to do so. The novelty of rapid change no less than its significance had deeply impressed thoughtful people contemplating an era that began by applauding *Frankenstein* and ended by
avidly buying Wells's *The Time Machine* (1895), *The Island of Doctor
Moreau* (1896), *The Invisible Man* (1897), *The War of the Worlds*
(1898), *Tales of Space and Time* (1899), and *The First Men in the
Moon* (1901). The nineteenth century offers abundant evidence to
support those who define science fiction most simply but with
perfect accuracy as the literature of change.

To an author of tales about invasion from Mars and travel to
the moon writing sober *Anticipations* two years before Orville
and Wilbur Wright flew at Kitty Hawk, change was the grand
fact of the modern world. It was change, moreover, most conspicuously manifested via "mechanical and scientific progress."
Throughout the book of prophecy that features those words in
its title, Wells specifies "the enormous development of mechanism which has been the cardinal feature of the nineteenth
century" (*Anticipations*, 66). The symbol of this era, Wells suggests, should be "a steam engine running upon a railway"
(*Anticipations*, 4).

Improvement of locomotion via the steamship and railroad
marked for Wells a decisive break with the previous condition of
civilization. Only the Roman corn ships offered anything comparable, but they were in his view hardly of equal magnitude or
consequences. Even more drastic breaks with the stay-at-home
past clearly lay just ahead via the development of aviation.
Humanity's perennial dream of flight had been achieved by the
Montgolfier balloon in 1783, to be followed by intermittent military applications, experiments with dirigible airships, and persistent work toward what in prospect no less than in retrospect
seemed the inevitable achievement of heavier-than-air flying
machines. Wells did not foresee much development of passenger
aircraft but like many others imagined with an odd mixture of
gloom and relish the potentialities of aerial warfare. In 1899 he
ended *When the Sleeper Wakes* with a vivid scene of combat

between a fighter plane and troop transports. From this it was an easy leap to space flight. Nor was Wells alone in appreciating the imaginative appeal as well as the social impact of fast travel, and indeed of all kinds of travel. For science fiction, "getting there" has always been half the fun and perhaps more than half of the necessary inspiration.

The literary consequences of the nineteenth century's transportation revolution are striking in a list of only a few of Jules Verne's "voyages extraordinaires" by which he helped to found science fiction: *Five Weeks in a Balloon* (1863); *Journey to the Center of the Earth* (1864); *From the Earth to the Moon* (1865); *Around the Moon* (1870); *Twenty Thousand Leagues Under the Sea* (1870); *Around the World in Eighty Days* (1873); *The Steam House* (1880); *The Giant Raft* (1881); *The Clipper of the Clouds* (1886); *Propeller Island* (1895); and *The Aerial Village* (1901). Whether all of these count equally as science fiction matters less than the prominence of transportation as a link connecting more or less realistic adventure narratives to tales of space flight, air ships, and futuristic submarines. Travel writing since long before Homer's *Odyssey* had been appealing whether recounting real voyages, imaginary voyages, or combinations of fact and fancy. Explorers sailing in the wake of Columbus very much stimulated the literature of voyaging after 1492. But it was only in the nineteenth century that actual possibilities of locomotion at last outpaced the literary imagination and turned it in new directions.

This could happen because there were well-developed forms awaiting the catalyst that would change their shape. A utopian scheme of travel to a better society, based in turn on the conventional framework of a returned traveler recounting his adventures, provides the basis for *Gulliver's Travels*, as for so much later science fiction in the Swiftian mode. Another precursor of science fiction, of which indeed *Gulliver's Travels* is also partly an example, is the Robinsonade, so called after Daniel Defoe's *Robinson Crusoe* (1719), which tells the story of a man stranded in an alien environment who must cope with its dangers and opportunities while wrestling with the problems of isolation by bringing to bear the spiritual, intellectual, and material resources of the civilization from which he came. Montesquieu's *Lettres persanes* (*Persian Letters*) of 1721 effectively inaugurated the idea of bringing foreign observers to Europe to provide a defamiliarizing account of it rather than sending Europeans to strange places elsewhere. Voltaire's *Micromégas* (1752) takes this notion in a more science fictional direction while also engaging in Swiftian dramatization of relativity by bringing to earth for commentary on our society giant inhabitants from the star Sirius and the planet Saturn. Like Swift's huge king of Brobdingnag, they of course find humanity not only small but petty. Even the space voyage had become a staple of travel literature by the eighteenth century, used most beautifully as well as to the most telling satiric effects by Cyrano de Bergerac in *L'autre monde* (*The Other World*), first published in 1657 as *Histoire comique des états et empires de la lune* (*Comic History of the States and Empires of the Moon*). To this established tradition of imaginary voyages Verne and kindred science fiction writers stimulated by the transportation revolution brought new heights of realism, zest, and relevance in dealing with the *modes* of travel.

But more is involved than mere fascination with present and future transport for its own sake as an engineering marvel. Many of Verne's vehicles, as Arthur Evans has remarked, are mobile utopias in miniature: cozy havens within which travelers venturing through dangerous environments experience a better life than they had while at rest.[15] In other ways too, science fiction travel in the Vernian tradition provides new vantage points for utopian or dystopian commentary on life at home in the reader's city. Equally important, the appeal of such tales for readers and writers alike was enhanced by their provision of ways to cope mentally with the rapid urbanization that was a claustrophobic result of better transportation. Verne provides grand models of escape from the city into what readers if not his protagonists may regard as more pastoral arenas such as outer space and the ocean's depths. Dystopian portraits of the megalopolis itself, so familiar now in works like *Neuromancer* and *Blade Runner*, have as one model Wells's oppressive future city in *When the Sleeper Wakes*. In *Anticipations* he observed also that railroads had led to the crowding together of people in cities whose gigantic size was for the Western world "entirely an unprecedented thing" (*Anticipations*, 34). The megalopolis is a characteristic feature of modern times to which science fiction from Jules Verne forward is an equally characteristic response.

The other great nineteenth-century transformation identified by Wells in *Anticipations* is the intellectual revolution foreshadowed in 1798 by Thomas Malthus in *An Essay on the Principle of Population* and precipitated in 1859 by publication of Charles Darwin's *On the Origin of Species by Means of Natural Selection*. The hornet's nest of controversy stirred up by Darwin's alternative to the biblical account of creation has not even yet quieted down, and it is therefore more familiar now than the uproar created by Malthus's no less relevant warning that population increase will lead to catastrophe if not severely checked. But to Wells writing in 1901 it seemed that "probably no more shattering book than the *Essay on Population* has ever been, or ever will be, written" because it rendered futile "all dreams of earthly golden ages" that might be achieved by "social reconstruction" without draconian population control; and because it helped inspire Darwin's research, thus setting "such forces in motion as have destroyed the very root-ideas of orthodox righteousness in the Western world" (*Anticipations*, 288–89). To Wells looking back on the period during which he and others brought science fiction to prominence, the undoubted material benefits of better transportation that had been accompanied by the more dubious features of inescapable urbanization and increasing secularization were matched psychologically not by sanguine confidence in further progress but by "shattering" anxieties about the loss of religious certainties. It is clear enough, although Wells does not spell this out, that such pessimism creates fertile ground for the growth of literary forms like science fiction that can effectively address the philosophical issues no less than the material conditions accompanying the new anxieties.

Wells understood the other scientific currents that contributed their share to nineteenth-century anxiety. Proliferation during the seventeenth century and afterward of the microscope and telescope led to better but hardly reassuring understanding of our place in the grand scale of things. These instruments also stimulated wider acknowledgment of the relativity of those very scales by which size is measured. New theories of astronomy removed our planet and its inhabitants from the center of the universe while identifying too its vast inhuman size. Telescopes allowed contemplation of an apparently endless vista of stars beyond our solar system. To this immensity Blaise Pascal, in his

Pensées (*Thoughts*) of 1670, eloquently articulated an uneasy reaction, which has echoed in science fiction ever since: "The silence of those infinite spaces terrifies me."

To alarming awareness of the apparently unpopulated and mostly empty infinity beyond our solar system, geology added more immediately disquieting glimpses of the earth's age, implying a past and also a future that might in effect be equally infinite rather than comfortably bounded by the biblical story of Creation at one end of time and Apocalypse at the other. While the interval between these events remained indefinite, it was nevertheless easily imaginable to those who accepted creation as a week's work and the universe as not much more than four thousand years old. Starting with Buffon's *Epoques de la nature* in 1779 such comfortably low estimates became increasingly untenable, as did the first chapters of Genesis, which Charles Darwin threatened to dispose of altogether. Moreover, as Sylvia K. Miller suggests, the temporal infinity ahead no longer offered a soothing prospect of duplicating the past but instead generated fear of the unknown: "The future was at one time predictable and recognizable because all of history was seen as a cycle in which mankind would journey forth only to return to its origins, having destroyed prelapsarian innocence at the Fall only to recover it at the Apocalypse. Darwin and science in general seem to have broken this time circle and transformed it into an open-ended line."[16] Wells unerringly and vividly identifies the most important consequence of all this: "In conjunction with the wide vistas opened by geological and astronomical discovery, the nineteenth century has indeed lost the very habit of thought from which the belief in a Fall arose. *It is as if a hand had been put upon the head of the thoughtful man and had turned his eyes about from the past to the future*" (*Anticipations*, 290; emphasis added).

This wonderfully Swiftian image of a giant hand turning humanity around to face its future epitomizes the change most important for science fiction. Not all of it, to be sure, is or need be set in the future. Neither *Frankenstein*, for example, nor Jules Verne's major novels are placed ahead in time. But without that possibility as a formal resource, and without an audience disposed to look ahead rather than to the past, science fiction could never have achieved anything like its full powers. The allegory of *Animal Farm* might have been the uttermost limit of even

Orwell's genius if he had not been able to write *Nineteen Eighty-Four*. Had he lived three centuries earlier there would have been no precedents to encourage anything like such a work, nor any audience disposed to read it. Before 1659, when Jacques Guttin published *Epigone, histoire du siècle futur* (Epigone, a story of the future century), there were no secular narratives set in future time. Writers from antiquity to the Renaissance never tried future settings. If they ever considered the possibility, it did not interest them. But after *Epigone* broke the taboo there followed in the eighteenth century a significant number of similar efforts, starting in 1733 with Samuel Madden's *Memoirs of the Twentieth Century*. Most notable among these pioneering experiments with futuristic fiction is the first utopia set ahead in time rather than on some imaginary island: Louis-Sébastien Mercier's widely read *L'An 2440* (The year 2440), a utopian vision of twenty-fifth century Paris published in 1771. Thanks in large part to Mercier's influential best-seller, the tale of the future became an established genre by 1850. As with the imaginary voyage and Gothic fiction, but even more crucially, the prior invention of futuristic fiction made possible the full development of science fiction. What brought this genre into being was, as for all literature, partly the inexplicable gift of genius displayed by the likes of Mary Shelley, Jules Verne, and H. G. Wells. It was partly the rich legacy of previous, especially eighteenth-century, formal experimentation. Above all it was the acceleration of intellectual and material change that resulted in turning humanity away from myths of its past to dreams of its future.

2

England: New Viewpoints

The event on which the interest of the story depends . . . however impossible as a physical fact, affords a point of view to the imagination for the delineating of human passions more comprehensive and commanding than any which the ordinary relations of existing events can yield.

"Preface" to *Frankenstein*

Mary Shelley: Frankenstein

Like *Frankenstein*, the best science fiction offers alternative viewpoints to the reader's imagination and stresses consequences rather than techniques of science. Within previous English literature the most significant feature for the development of science fiction is a remarkably successful quest for new points of view. During the century before *Frankenstein*, English writers vigorously sought fresh temporal, spatial, and psychological vantage points from which to contemplate the human condition. Of course their efforts had precedents. Historians of science fiction usually single out among imaginary voyages, for example, a long tradition of planetary travel inaugurated in the second century A.D. by satirical episodes on the moon included in Lucian of Samosata's *True History* and *Icaro-Menippus*. Inspired by this model, English writers too sent travelers to the moon where earthly life could be seen from a defamiliarizing distance. The most popular of their early extraterrestrial fantasies, read attentively by Jules Verne and Edgar Allan Poe among others, was Francis Godwin's *Man in the Moone; or, A Discourse of a Voyage Thither by Domingo Gonsales* (1638). In *Iter Lunare; or, A Voyage to the Moon* (1703) David Russen provided a critique of Cyrano de Bergerac's *Comic History of the States and Empires of the Moon* (1657). Of themselves, however, lunar and planetary excursions following Lucian's trajectory were something of a dead end, leading mainly to similar fantasies that did not much point attention toward science, toward the future, or toward more effective techniques of cognitive estrangement. By dwelling mostly in the timeless realm of myth, such works deflected attention alike from the future and from new methods of defamiliarizing the present. More relevant to science fiction than utopian or satiric recourse to the moon and remote planets are the ways in which eighteenth-century English writers varied available genres to create those new perspectives afforded by the Robinsonade, historical fiction, and the psychological novel.

Bernard Bergonzi's description of the narrative structure common to *The Time Machine* and other early scientific romances by H. G. Wells could also be a definition of the Robinsonade created by Defoe: "a character is transferred to or marooned in a wholly alien environment, and the story arises from his efforts to deal with the situation."[1] Before Daniel Defoe published *Robinson Crusoe* in 1719, no one, not even those who sent their travelers out to the moon and beyond, had imagined anything like Crusoe's long solitude. It is from this unusual perspective that Defoe invites readers to contemplate afresh every aspect of their civilization from its religion to its chairs, tables, and ways of making bread. The effects are those of cognitive estrangement. Defoe's account of how Crusoe deals with isolation in an adverse environment is equally notable for the ways in which it focuses on attitudes toward the alien other as well as the alien landscape. Paradoxically, Defoe treats this theme most brilliantly without resort to extraterrestrials or space travel, although he too had done apprentice work in the Lucianic tradition by publishing lunar voyages, of which the best known during his lifetime was *The Consolidator; or, Memoirs of Sundry Transactions from the World in the Moon* (1705). Perhaps his experiments of this kind persuaded Defoe of their limitations while stimulating him to think of alternatives. In any event, it is neither his obscure lunar satires nor others like them that have been most often remembered and imitated by science fiction writers, but *Robinson Crusoe*. It is not Defoe's moon-dwellers or their Selenite predecessors but human cannibals who provide one of the most influential alien encounters in world literature. The "print of a man's naked foot" whose discovery terrifies Crusoe—and which has reappeared with variations in science fiction and even in pictures of Neil Armstrong's footprints on the moon—symbolizes a presence that is both human and alien: human because it is left by a person anatomically like himself, but alien because that person is imagined to be altogether different culturally and therefore inevitably hostile. Ironically, the cannibal rescued by Crusoe becomes a good Christian and pleasant companion as well as a helpful servant. Whatever the shortcomings of Friday's conversion as a paradigm for coping with threatening differences, *Robinson Crusoe* provided a positive model of how the alien may be assimilated rather than simply despised or destroyed.

Defoe's other great contribution to the resources of science fiction is *A Journal of the Plague Year* (1722), an imaginary eyewitness account of London's devastation in 1665 by the bubonic plague. *A Journal of the Plague Year* achieves a power akin to that of much science fiction, because it shows people encountering something inhuman that (given the science of their day) can neither be understood nor assimilated peacefully. The disease plays the role of an alien that is genuinely other and truly hostile. Mary Shelley's second science fiction novel, *The Last Man* (1826), reflects Defoe's influence by its portrait of a far more devastating plague set in a twenty-first-century future when the sole survivor left on earth eloquently laments that his isolation is worse than Crusoe's: "He was far happier than I: for he could hope, nor hope in vain—the destined vessel at last arrived, to bear him to countrymen and kindred, where the events of his solitude became a fire-side tale. To none could I ever relate the story of my adversity. . . . Beneath the meridian sun and visiting moon, I alone bore human features. . . . He had fled from his fellows, and was transported with terror at the print of a human foot. I would have knelt down and worshipped the same."[2] Defoe's early impact on the science fictional imagination is clearly attested here. In *The Last Man*, Mary Shelley combines features of *Robinson Crusoe* and *A Journal of the Plague Year* while displacing their plots to a future setting and managing also to create as a challenge for her successors an apparent *ne plus ultra* in the line of isolation and devastation.

Defoe's vivid portrait of a city under siege by nonhuman forces inspired too H. G. Wells's account of havoc wreaked by Martians in *The War of the Worlds* (1898), which in turn has served as the archetype for a whole subspecies of science fiction in which disaster arrives from outer space. After noting (as others have) this strong influence of Defoe on Wells, Anthony Burgess remarks that "when post-Wellsian science fiction presents its collective horrors—either in words or on film—Defoe is somewhere in the background. *Robinson Crusoe* and the *Journal* are the prototypes of all imaginative works that show man, individually and collectively, facing the horrible and unexpected."[3] As pioneering historical fiction, moreover, *A Journal of the Plague Year* is one harbinger of a profound change that occurred when novelists began to explore the possibilities of turning for settings to the past and the future. In 1765 Horace Walpole's *Castle of Otranto* initiated the vogue of Gothic fiction that was another forerunner of the historical novel elaborated in the nineteenth century by Sir Walter Scott and his imitators. In addition to the affinities of Gothic and science fiction in their quest for sublimity that I noted in chapter 1, the key feature of Gothic fiction was its emphasis on the past. This contributed to the liberation of novelists from imaginative confinement to the present or the atemporal realms of "once upon a time" that sufficed to locate the action of so much fantasy. Time became a significant arena within which perspectives could be varied.

So did the mind. Science fiction is too often associated only with voyages outward to the moon and beyond. Its attention to the inner spaces of human psychology is equally significant but has been less often remarked except in connection with trends of French science fiction after World War II and as a prominent concern of Anglophone writers from the 1960s New Wave forward, especially in the fiction of Philip K. Dick, in such tours-de-force as Frederik Pohl's *Gateway* (1977), and in variations on the mental landscapes of William Gibson's cyberspace. Mary Shelley, however, turned science fiction inward at its creation by focusing so much on the states of mind of her characters while playing off those states of mind against one another to involve readers in the subjective dimensions of the tale she tells. Although English Romanticism from the 1790s onward was a powerful philosophical stimulus to this introspective turn, the most important narrative model was doubtless Samuel Richardson's *Clarissa* of 1747–48. It inaugurated the psychological novel by its notorious subordination of action to sentiment; by the sheer extent of its concern with the heroine's inner life; and even more significantly by its structure as an epistolary novel in which many of the same events are recounted by various characters from their own points of view without the intrusion of an omniscient author. In all this Richardson too had precedents, but in developing them into a new kind of novel he offered more in *Clarissa* for Mary Shelley's creative use than any moon voyage had.

For those who come to *Frankenstein*, as most twentieth-century readers do, after first seeing cinematic versions ranging from Boris Karloff's classic to *The Rocky Horror Picture Show*, the most surprising features of Mary Shelley's text are likely to be its multiplicity of narrators, including the monster himself, and its elaborate descriptions of arctic and alpine landscapes. Almost equally surprising may be the characters featured in subordinate plots: Robert Walton the arctic explorer; the De Lacey family together with Felix De Lacey's exotic Turkish fiancée Saphie; and Justine Moritz. These complications create many perspectives. Only one version of events is usually provided by films, although a few, like *Rashomon* (1950), may go over the same incident from different angles, thereby leaving viewers to decide what really happened as well as what to make of it. Even more rarely do films present anything but an external vantage point: that of the camera. At the movies we almost always see everybody from outside. As Norman Spinrad notes with the proprietary relief of a skillful science fiction writer contemplating one distinct advantage remaining to the printed page, "You can do a lot of things in film that you can't do in prose fiction, but one thing you *can't* do is put the audience inside a character's head."[4] Not effectively, that is. Written narratives more easily portray events as they appear through the eyes of participants. It is this subjectivity that Mary Shelley exploits to superb effect by putting us inside both Frankenstein and his monster.

The primary narrator of *Frankenstein* is twenty-eight-year-old Robert Walton, who is writing a journal in the form of letters to his sister Margaret Saville about a strange encounter while leading a voyage of exploration toward the North Pole, where he hopes to "tread a land never before imprinted by the foot of man."[5] Walton's account of his mathematical and medical studies identifies him as a scientist. Readers may also see him as an unbalanced dreamer when they learn that Walton has led his crew into dangerous waters—from which they finally demand that he turn back—motivated not merely by the old chimera of discovering a Northwest Passage but also by less plausible utopian visions of the pole as a land of unsurpassed beauty, eternal light, and perpetual warmth. Walton cannot accept more usual (and accurate) ideas of Arctic regions as "the seat of frost and desolation" (*F*, 15). Shelley ingeniously echoes Robinson Crusoe's discovery of the footprint by making Walton perversely as well as bravely long to go where there is no such sign that anyone has gone before. Though he only puts it symbolically via his image of being the first to tread the polar region, Walton's figure of speech reveals that he longs to be the initial alien presence there, leaving prints for others to find. In this, however, he is disappointed because far across menacing icefields that have closed in on his ship he glimpses one day the "strange sight" of a dog-sledge carrying a figure shaped like a man but of gigantic size. To Walton (again distantly echoing *Robinson Crusoe*) the figure looks like "a savage inhabitant of some undiscovered island" (*F*, 23). But this is no easily converted Man Friday offering pleasant companionship. It is Victor Frankenstein's monster, as Walton eventually discovers. Our introduction to the creature is from a distance seen through telescopes by Walton and his crew as it mysteriously recedes northward over the hostile landscape of arctic ice. What is it? Where has it come from? Why is it making its way toward the North Pole?

These questions are only answered after Walton rescues an exhausted and dying Victor Frankenstein from an ice floe the next day and thereafter hears his story of why he is pursuing the monster. Walton's transcription of Frankenstein's autobiographical narration occupies most of Shelley's text, which ends with a resumption of the letters to Margaret Saville by way of conclusion as Walton describes Frankenstein's death followed by the monster's dramatic appearance on the ship to pronounce a self-justifying soliloquy over his creator's corpse. The monster has the novel's last word in this speech, bitterly condemning his creator along with the human race. Instead of either refuting these allegations or agreeing with them by way of providing a final moral to the tale, Walton enigmatically closes his narrative in symmetry with its initial episode by simply recording a last sight of the monster seen from afar heading north again to disappear "in darkness and distance" (F, 211). An important question, accordingly, is how Frankenstein's account was received by its first audience, Walton. His sympathetic interpretation may not be a model for subsequent readers.

Frankenstein's structure of nested narrations with final words from the monster challenges readers to answer for themselves—since there is no omniscient author to do it for them—even more crucial questions about how Walton or anyone *should* respond. Is he right to like Frankenstein so much while hesitating to condemn his new friend's disastrous experiment? Is Victor Frankenstein no worse than Walton describes him, an "ill-fated and admirable" figure dogged by bad luck as well as some mistakes in judgment (F, 207)? Was he meddling with things better left alone or merely going about worthwhile experiments the wrong way? If he is "The Modern Prometheus" as *Frankenstein's* subtitle states, are we to take this parallel as a compliment to Frankenstein because it implies that he was attempting something as noble as Prometheus's theft of fire from the gods for humanity's benefit? Or should we take the parallel as ironic condemnation of a modern world where self-deluded scientists who regard themselves as Promethean benefactors in reality provide only dangerous monstrosities? Science fiction is too often mistaken for a literature of prophecy best measured by the accuracy of its predictions, whereas it is better judged as *Frankenstein* invites judgment, by its ability to pose challenging questions about the human condition in an age of science.

Victor Frankenstein is quick to see Walton as a younger version of himself: "You seek for knowledge and wisdom, as I once did" (F, 28). The equation of Walton and Frankenstein as scientists alike pursuing knowledge, although in different fields, is underscored within Frankenstein's account by explicit emphasis on his scientific education at the University of Ingolstadt. Before arriving there from his home in Geneva the precocious but untutored Victor read widely in what he only later realized were the "exploded systems" of Cornelius Agrippa, Paracelsus, Albertus Magnus, and the like. Fascinated by the promises of alchemy and magic the gullible young Frankenstein was eager to raise "ghosts or devils" (F, 40). At Ingolstadt his professors are amazed that he has wasted time "studying such nonsense" and turn his enthusiasm away from "the dreams of forgotten alchemists" to modern science (F, 45–46). He concentrates on anatomy, physiology, and especially chemistry, inspired by Professor Waldman's visionary panegyric on what chemists have achieved: "These philosophers, whose hands seem only made to dabble in dirt, and their eyes to pore over the microscope or crucible, have indeed performed miracles. They penetrate into the recesses of nature and show how she works in her hiding-places. They ascend into the heavens; they have discovered how the blood circulates, and the nature of the air we breathe. They have acquired new and almost unlimited powers; they can command the thunders of heaven, mimic the earthquake, and even mock the invisible world with its own shadows" (F, 47). In retrospect Frankenstein sees these as the words that lured him to his doom by arousing ambition to perform his own scientific "miracles." By including this very precise history of Frankenstein's education Mary Shelley suggests fatal parallels between old dreams of raising demons and new dreams of scientific discovery.

She also thereby invites a reading of Frankenstein as a variation on the Faust legend: an up-to-date version of that fable of a learned man who rashly sells his soul to the devil in return for knowledge and power. Certainly if Victor Frankenstein is in some sense a modern Prometheus, he is also a modern Faust. By direct and implied allusion to these archetypes Shelley greatly enhances Frankenstein's mythic force. To stress only such parallels, however, as some do, is to reduce Frankenstein to nothing more than a modern-dress presentation of familiar legends, with the monster accordingly dismissed as only one more demon or golem conjured into being by yet another wicked magician. If taken as a sufficient account of *Frankenstein*, this interpretation is too reductive. Frankenstein's chemistry professor is at most an accidental Mephistopheles who fades out of the narration apparently unaware that his speech led Frankenstein disastrously astray. No one wants his soul, nor does he worry much about damnation. The most significant point of Mary Shelley's emphasis on Frankenstein's education is that he has *left* the realm of magicians and Faustian compacts, that is to say the realm of fairy tale and fable—and theism—for the secular outlook of modern science.[6]

To describe scientific achievements as miracles is to speak metaphorically, not literally. To call Frankenstein a modern Prometheus or Faust is also to speak metaphorically, which is not to say inconsequentially or incorrectly. But the meaning of such metaphors resides after all in the differences no less than the similarities between tenor and vehicle. What makes Victor Frankenstein not merely echo but displace Faust as the archetypal figure of our age is precisely realization that what we may carelessly or poetically describe as the "miracles" of modern science are brought about by human, not supernatural, agency. Allusion to knowledge of the blood's circulation and the air's composition is a reminder that scientific experimentation of the kind symbolized by Frankenstein's creation of the monster may lead to drastic consequences in a purely material world. Though what he does is not yet possible, it stands for a class of activities that *are* possible thanks to science. Frankenstein's animation of the monster must therefore be referred to reality in a way ultimately different from the mimesis of ghost stories or even the ethical dilemmas of the Faust legend. Mary Shelley's careful delineation of Victor Frankenstein's progress from Geneva to Ingolstadt, from childhood dabblings in alchemy and magic to adult use—and misuse—of science, takes her story over the threshold separating ancient and modern, superstition and science. It takes her book over the border from fantasy to science fiction.

Frankenstein's dying words, spoken to a fellow scientist, are an ambivalent warning that reveals his own incorrigible uncertainty about the implications of his scientific misadventure: "Farewell, Walton! Seek happiness in tranquillity and avoid ambition, even if it be only the apparently innocent one of distinguishing yourself in science and discoveries. Yet why do I say this? I have myself been blasted in these hopes, yet another may succeed" (F, 206). Shortly before this valediction that suggests two very different morals for his tale, Frankenstein rallies his strength for a noble speech urging Walton's crew to persist hero- ically in their voyage northward despite its dangers and so become glorious "benefactors of your species" even if necessary at the expense of their lives (F, 203). The men are not persuaded. Walton perforce abandons his mission while blaming them for cowardice. Readers may be more inclined to applaud the crew as realistic and condemn Walton for so readily accepting Frankenstein's outlook by valuing scientific discovery over a prudent regard for human life. Walton may thus be regarded as the first misreader of Frankenstein's story, seduced by his self- serving rhetoric of apology. We must decide. Interpretative chal- lenges posed by the interplay of Frankenstein and Walton at the novel's beginning and end define central themes. By suggesting that Frankenstein's apparently unique predicament actually poses questions equally relevant for other scientists, starting with Walton, Shelley enhances *Frankenstein*'s philosophical scope as well as its dramatic interest.

Her most telling engagement of readers via alteration of per- spectives is achieved by the surprising strategy of including within Victor Frankenstein's narrative as told to Walton the monster's account of his life as told to Victor Frankenstein when they meet amid the "sublime" setting of "the mighty Alps, whose white and shining pyramids and domes towered above all, as belonging to another earth, the habitations of another race of beings" (F, 90). Like the Arctic landscapes within which *Frankenstein* opens and closes, this alpine scenery reinforces the novel's effects of sublimity while inviting readers to contemplate their ephemeral civilization from the distant perspective of an eternal though inhuman natural order. Shelley's description of this scenery also evokes an estranging view of our world as though it were a different planet inhabited by "another race of beings." Awesome backdrops of snow-covered mountains and polar icefields at the edge of space thus enhance our sense of the monster as alien by placing him in what amounts to an extrater- restrial setting. Shelley has it both ways. Her characters stay on earth, but we are told to imagine our world as another planet.

And in doing so we may feel a tremor of Pascalian terror at the eternal silence of those infinite spaces beyond our orbit.

Allusions within *Frankenstein* to Coleridge's *Rime of the Ancient Mariner* and Wordsworth's *Tintern Abbey* evoke two ways of regarding nature: as the menacing and eerie setting of the ancient mariner's horrifying adventure (in which Walton finds disquieting affinities with his own situation); and as a comforting source of pleasure combined with a kind of religious veneration. It is hard to read *Frankenstein* as espousing the latter view when the monster kills Frankenstein's friend Henry Clerval, whose love of nature is described by the quotation from *Tintern Abbey* (*F*, 149). Clerval's death is a rejection of Wordsworthian optimism about nature. The lifeless cold of mountains and icecaps, standing symbolically for other worlds as well as for the forces of nature that constrain us on this one, plays off against the flickering existence of Shelley's protagonists as Frankenstein dies aboard Walton's ship, the monster announces there his plan to destroy himself on a great funeral pyre in the northern solitudes, and Walton turns back from further exploration to save his vessel from being crushed amid the ice floes. The best way to appreciate the potentialities for science fiction of what Shelley so richly accomplishes with the landscapes of *Frankenstein* is to read Ursula K. Le Guin's beautiful account in *The Left Hand of Darkness* (1969) of Genly Ai's trip with Estraven across the planet Gethen's icefields.

Frankenstein's readers are invited to shift perspectives radically by seeing events through the monster's eyes only *after* hearing from Frankenstein of his revulsion at creating such an ugly thing, his immediate abandonment of it, and of its subsequent horrible vengeance on Frankenstein's family by murdering his young brother William and planting evidence that causes Justine Moritz to be executed for a crime she did not commit. Not until we have been allowed to share Victor Frankenstein's outrage at all this do we discover why the monster did such things. We find that he has understandable if not sufficient motives. By this unexpected shift in perspective, which is not at all necessary for the expository purpose of presenting the external action of *Frankenstein*—what a camera could record—Mary Shelley turns into a psychological masterpiece what otherwise might indeed have been little more than a modern-dress version of the Faust legend with the addition of a monster that everybody would love to hate—the perfect script for a B movie. But *Frankenstein* becomes far better than this by virtue of the monster's autobiography.

He elicits our sympathy with an account of his suffering at the hands of humans whom he befriends and wishes to love but who viciously reject him only because they deem him ugly. If in his initial inclination to virtue he plays the familiar role of noble savage, his tragedy is that he is not encountered on some remote island where differences are to be expected, but turned loose by his irresponsible creator in the midst of an intolerant civilization that regards domestic deviation from its norms simply as despicable monstrosity. He is not offered Friday's opportunity for conversion, but is forced to remain an alien. No one thinks of calling him anything but "monster," "devil," or "filthy demon." He never even acquires the dignity of a name. Through his narrative we can vicariously experience the pain of being persecuted on account of superficial differences.

There is an obvious but important moral here, which, like that derived from the execution of Justine Moritz, becomes a strong indictment of both human nature and human society. While Shelley's text hardly endorses Victor Frankenstein's brand of rebellious creativity, neither does it paint an appealing picture of alternatives within the social world that created *him*. Its representatives are as quick as he to perceive difference as unacceptable monstrosity. They are even quicker to persecute the powerless. If read as a political fable with the monster representing oppressed lower classes dangerously turning to revolutionary violence, *Frankenstein* is remarkable not for doctrinaire stands for or against revolution in general or the French Revolution in particular—topics at which it glances ambiguously—but for its highly original narrative of oppression viewed from the perspective of the oppressed.[7] The social criticism that is one hallmark of science fiction at its best is a prominent feature of *Frankenstein*.

Readers must grapple with the question of how far if at all the monster's mistreatment by humans excuses him from blame for the revenge killings not only of William and (indirectly) Justine but also of Henry Clerval and Frankenstein's bride Elizabeth, murdered on her wedding night. How much responsibility for these crimes can be shifted from the monster to the man who created but abandoned him without any ethical (or other) education and then finally refused even to create a mate who could have relieved the monster's solitude? The difficulty of this question prevents sympathy for either the monster or Frankenstein from devolving into sentimentality. So does the monster's strong identification with Satan after he reads Milton's *Paradise Lost*. This affinity also works to counteract any merely sentimental pity aroused by the monster's rather maudlin though understandable feeling of kinship with the suicidally sensitive protagonist of Goethe's *Sorrows of Young Werther*, who is more prosaically deprived of a mate. Sympathy for unhappy lovers or outcasts, even criminal outcasts of Satanic inclinations, is a feature of *Frankenstein's* Romantic context that Shelley skillfully exploits to enhance her novel's ethical complexity. However readers resolve its dilemmas, both Frankenstein and the monster have undeniably done terrible things. What makes the book so compelling is not primarily the moral conundrums posed for our consideration by its plot, worthwhile as it is to debate such matters, but the way in which shifting perspectives of first-person narratives by Frankenstein and the monster allow readers the imaginative leap of placing themselves for a while into the heads of each to see their situation from the inside as well as the outside.

Even more significant as a science fictional technique is the cognitive estrangement achieved by inviting readers to see their own world as it appears to an intelligent alien. While the monster proceeds with its account readers find themselves engaged in a double take of first trying to grasp the outlook of a being whose experience seems utterly unlike their own and then trying to cope with a growing realization that affinities do exist. We come to see *ourselves* as aliens—and rather unpleasant ones at that—from the monster's point of view while recognizing with increasing discomfort that he, the archetypal alien if ever there was one from our point of view, is in too many ways exactly like ourselves mentally though not physically. Swift's alien Houyhnhnms, who are seen only from the outside through Gulliver's eyes, remain so aloofly rational that readers (unlike Gulliver) cannot easily identify with them even if abstractly agreeing with their judgment that humans are worse than Yahoos. Shelley collapses the distinction between alien and human although not by Defoe's method of assimilating the alien to ourselves as in Crusoe's conversion of Friday, but by the opposite method of assimilating ourselves to the alien. The stinger is that we are then inclined emotionally as well as rationally to share in the alien's revulsion at humanity, i.e., ourselves.

After describing his initial sensations upon first coming into existence and living in a preverbal state—a period that may seem to readers like an evocation of their own or any person's infancy described with adult sensibility—the monster tells of learning first to speak and then to read while hiding out where he secretly observes the De Lacey family in their cottage. By elaborating this part of his account far beyond the plot requirement that the monster somehow acquire speech, Shelley invites readers to consider the humanizing role of language, which is usually as much taken for granted as the air we breathe. The injustices of human society that we ignore with equal ease are singled out for consideration as the monster pieces together the De Lacey family history of falling into poverty because of acting like Good Samaritans in rescuing from a Parisian jail an unjustly imprisoned Turkish merchant who subsequently betrays them. This provides a microhistory of human society stressing the triumph of selfishness over virtue. A macrohistory is supplied via the book that along with *Paradise Lost* (1667) and *The Sorrows of Young Werther* (1774) completes the monster's accidental education: Volney's *Ruins of Empires* (*Les Ruines, ou meditations sur les révolutions des empires*, 1719). In this panorama of history the monster finds many "noble and godlike" people to admire but weeps over Volney's account of "the discovery of the American hemisphere and . . . the hapless fate of its original inhabitants" (*F*, 114). By these tears Shelley identifies the monster with another oppressed group, native peoples dispossessed by Europeans. He finally turns away from Volney's many episodes of "vice and bloodshed" with "disgust and loathing" (*F*, 114). As outside observer (playing now the role of noble savage turned *philosophe*), this is the monster's final judgment on the human race. Should it be ours?

Again the answer matters less—though it *does* matter—than the estranged perspective here, which makes it hard to give the usual soothing replies to such a query. Other issues are raised from more oblique perspectives implied by *Frankenstein*'s symbolism. Shelley encourages remarkably varied but not mutually exclusive interpretations of her novel. Its initial reference to Prometheus points ambiguously toward one set of meanings. Another set is evoked by insistent allusions to *Paradise Lost*, also starting on *Frankenstein*'s title page, which challenge readers to decipher the even more ambiguous implications of inexact parallels between the monster and Adam as well as Satan, and between Victor Frankenstein and God. If he is God, although a God neither omniscient nor omnipotent who declines to create an Eve for his Adam and works natural rather than supernatural "miracles," does *Frankenstein* become a bleak allegory of human relationship to a deity who abandons his creation to evil? The book raises this question but does not fully answer it because its own story is so thoroughly secular, proceeding in ways that finally render theism and its attendant issues irrelevant without quite pronouncing the death of God.

Such questions are also hard to answer because *Frankenstein* hovers between allegory and realism without ever settling fully into either. It so conspicuously *lacks* verisimilitude at key points—such as association of the monster's animation with death and charnel houses—that Shelley's narrative proceeds with the illogical leaps more characteristic of dreams than of realistic novels, thereby inviting readers to seek symbolic significance for details rather than simply accepting them as enhancing plausibility. By having the monster vanish mysteriously for long intervals only to reappear with startling suddenness at such psychologically crucial moments as the wedding night, for example, Shelley invites us to see the creature as the destructive side of Victor Frankenstein, his alter ego. He himself recognizes the affinity by uneasily calling the monster "my own vampire, my own spirit let loose from the grave and forced to destroy all that was dear to me" (*F*, 74). But forced by whom? Frankenstein is, literally, the creator of his own torments. Viewed in this way, Frankenstein's struggle against the monster becomes the allegory of an inner combat of higher against baser instincts. Shelley thus provides the paradigm made most famous later in a simplified version by Robert Louis Stevenson's *Dr. Jekyll and Mr. Hyde* (1886), where a scientist turns into a monster by drinking a chemical potion.

To view the monster as Frankenstein's alter ego, that part of himself which is a "filthy demon" born of no woman who kills his bride on her wedding night, is also to recognize that *Frankenstein* covertly but jarringly deals with sexual relationships. Much has been written about Mary Shelley's own tangled attitudes toward these matters. Her mother Mary Wollstonecraft Godwin died shortly after Mary's birth, leaving to her daughter (who was later to write of a monster abandoned by its creator) the feminist legacy epitomized in *A Vindication of the Rights of Women* (1792). To whatever mixture of guilt, anger, and admiration that was provoked in Mary Shelley by the life and death of her mother were added ambivalent responses to William Godwin, a famous radical writer but far from a satisfactory father. By the time she wrote *Frankenstein*, Mary's attitudes toward sexual and parental relationships were also shaped by her stormy involvement with Percy Shelley along with her own experience of motherhood and the loss of a child. It is no wonder that psychoanalytical readings of *Frankenstein* occupy hundreds of disputatious pages to which I cannot do justice here beyond remarking two matters that have especially attracted such attention: Shelley focuses on males rather than females while presenting these males (Frankenstein and his monster) as responsible for the ill treatment and deaths of those women who most prominently enter the story (Justine Moritz and Elizabeth Lavenza); and Shelley conspicuously displaces women from the act of procreation while treating it as a filthy occurrence associated with death and parental irresponsibility.[8] What to make of this displacement must challenge every reader of *Frankenstein*.

For a history of science fiction the indisputable fact of overriding significance is that its founder was female. The genre begins by questioning patriarchy as represented by Victor Frankenstein and his murderous monster. Science fiction's first great story is rightly described by Peter Dale Scott as "essentially a feminist critique" in which "the symbolism works as well on the cultural level as on the personal, because Mary was able to expand her own personal responses to a dominating father, absent mother, and imbalanced husband into a compassionate study of an overly masculine society and its offspring."[9] In doing this Mary Shelley transformed the alienation experienced by women in a patriarchal society into a new myth apparently about males but of androgynous relevance to all readers. As a model for science fiction, the genre best suited to speak for and attract the marginalized, *Frankenstein*'s exemplary features include its female authorship and provocative subtext of feminist issues.

Interlude

Although the feminist potentialities of science fiction that Mary Shelley started to explore did not attract many women writers until the latter part of the twentieth century, one of the two most noteworthy English efforts between *Frankenstein* and the scientific romances of H. G. Wells was by another talented female: Jane Webb's *The Mummy: A Tale of the Twenty-Second Century* (1827). With a metafictional awareness that prefigures the self-consciousness of much later science fiction while also echoing Mary Shelley's account of trying to outdo previous ghost stories, Webb presents her book as a deliberate exercise in literary novelty aimed at finding a new kind of hero. Along with high romantic adventures revolving around the Irish King Roderick and his band of freedom fighters, Webb satirizes aspects of her own nineteenth-century world—especially its dawning faith in technological progress—by providing a cast of bumbling robot lawyers, robot judges, and robot surgeons as well as a comical mad scientist whose electrical experiments in Egypt revive the mummy of Cheops, who escapes in a dirigible to England where he spreads terror. Cheops resurrected in the future is indeed an original hero, who made *The Mummy* popular for reasons that Boris Karloff (using a different text) could later exploit even more fully. But without the possibilities of Hollywood, for which it was better suited than Shelley's masterpiece, *The Mummy* soon faded out of cultural memory. Webb's disappearance from literary history was unfortunately hastened by marriage to the landscape gardener John Claudius Loudon, who sought her out and proposed after reading *The Mummy*. Life with this ardent fan deflected Webb from science fiction to writing a series of botanical books with such unappealing titles as *The Ladies' Flower Garden of Ornamental Annuals*.

Webb describes Cheops's revival both as it appears to the frightened scientist unprepared for his experiment's success and to Cheops himself. Steamships on the Nile strike him as "strange infernal vessels, vomiting forth volumes of fire and smoke."[10] Nothing in sight corresponds to his memories of ancient Egypt or expectations of the afterlife. He does not know where—or when—he is. In these passages Webb achieves the unprecedented feat of showing how an imaginary future—which in its technological aspects is largely a metaphor of her reader's present—might be seen from the doubly estranging viewpoint of someone actually from a remote past. She thus invites readers to see their present as a contingent historical moment. But Webb does not sustain this skillful vignette of Cheops as time traveler whose ideas clash with experience of a totally alien future in ways that highlight the reader's differences from both past and future. After recovering from his initial bewilderment, Cheops operates at the level of magical fantasy rather than as an instance of the scientifically explained phenomenon of travel through time by means of galvanic resurrection from death. We no longer learn what he is thinking but see him only from the outside. Despite his initially menacing attitudes, he always acts to thwart the tale's villains while aiding its virtuous young lovers. His principle of action is out of the arbitrary world of fairy tale or Gothic novel. Fantasy prevails too when readers are finally told that it was not galvanism but God's will that actually brought Cheops back to life. Thus what seems like a scientific achievement turns out to have been a genuine miracle whose moral is clear: do not attempt to meddle with nature.

By treating that theme in a Gothic mode without recourse to the supernatural, *Frankenstein* became a prototype for science fiction as well as an enduring myth of the way in which science may destroy those who misuse it. *The Mummy* remains a comic fable without either tragic force, mythic power, or the cognitive interest that may be achieved by scientifically plausible marvels of the kind Félix Bodin was soon to call for and Jules Verne to achieve in his extraordinary voyages. *The Mummy* nevertheless deserves recognition because its future world is more skillfully subordinated to novelistic action than that of any previous futuristic fiction and because in it Jane Webb achieves a new viewpoint with immense potentialities for science fiction: that of a figure from the past confronting his and our future. The depicted future, and the reader's present, are thus seen simultaneously from two different vantage points.

A more immediately influential new perspective was offered by the other outstanding English work published in the interval between *Frankenstein* and the advent of H. G. Wells, George T.

Chesney's *The Battle of Dorking* (1871). This account of a future war in which Prussia invades and defeats England is one of those books whose idea is more important than its text. Previous tales of future warfare such as *The Reign of George VI 1900–1925* (1763) and Herbert Lang's *The Air Battle* (1859) had been set in what for their readers were remote futures. Chesney's great innovation was to set *The Battle of Dorking* in a very near future. Its vision of a defeated England thus implicated readers while gaining plausibility from France's loss of the Franco-Prussian War in the year of publication. Chesney's goal was to mobilize public opinion in favor of better armaments and more up-to-date tactics by portraying England's defeat as the result of inadequate military preparations. He stirred up public debate on this issue while also provoking a host of imitators, mostly English. The genre that Chesney created with *The Battle of Dorking* became something of an English specialty in the nineteenth century, although in the twentieth century America has taken the lead in mobilizing for impending future warfare. In *The New Ordeal* (1879), Chesney went on to stimulate the imaginative search for better weaponry by envisioning superbombs that would deter war. Intermediate between such utopian dreams of an ultimate weapon imposing peace and tales in which tactics of the last war are transferred to the next one are stories of the kind popularized by George Griffith's *The Angel of the Revolution* (1893). This account of a world war fought with submarines and airships imagines an advanced technology, thus providing a model for tales less focused on the current politics of military appropriations than stories closely imitating *The Battle of Dorking*. Of its nineteenth-century mutations, the most significant is of course H. G. Wells's *The War of the Worlds* (1898).

One reason for the scarcity of English science fiction during the interval between *Frankenstein* and the 1890s is the lack of outlets for shorter works. Three-volume novels—three-deckers— became the norm in England thanks to cooperation between publishers and circulating libraries. It was cheaper for people to pay a small fixed fee for annual unlimited borrowing privileges than to buy three-deckers at their rather considerable price. Popularity of the circulating libraries in turn provided a sufficiently profitable market for the three-deckers, thus discouraging publishers from those less expensive one-volume formats that were more available in America and France for writers like Poe and Verne. Noting these conditions of the literary marketplace, Brian Stableford persuasively argues that science fiction is most likely to flourish where shorter forms are available because "the sheer mass of detail required to flesh out a novel to three-volume length tied it down very firmly to the careful reproduction and analysis of known situations (present and past)."[11] In a talk on "Fiction about the Future" broadcast over Australian radio in 1938, H. G. Wells considered this difficulty for those who believe that serious novels are "the highest and most difficult form of futurist literature":

> The best sort of futurist story would be one that sets out to give you the illusion of reality. It ought to produce the effect of an historical novel, the other way round. It ought to read like fact. But alas, do any of us futurist writers ever get in sight of that much conviction? I'm afraid I must admit that none of us have ever succeeded in producing anything like the convincingness of hundreds of historical novels. No reader has ever *lived* in a futurist novel as we have all lived in the London of Dickens' *Barnaby Rudge* or the Paris of Hugo's *Notre Dame* or the Russia of Tolstoi's *War and Peace*. But then the historical romancer has a whole mass of history, ruins, old costumes, museum pieces, to work upon and confirm him; your minds are all ready furnished for him; the futurist writer has at most the bare germs of things to come and all your prejudices to surmount. He has to throw himself on your willingness to believe. You have to help him.[12]

Although Wells is far too modest about his own success, which lay very much in producing futures "that read like fact," these comments bear out Stableford's argument that longer forms impose the most daunting conditions on science fiction. It was therefore a happy coincidence that H. G. Wells turned to writing for his livelihood in the 1890s just as slender books and respectable periodicals willing to print short stories were replacing the stately three-decker.

H. G. Wells

Herbert George Wells (1866–1946) links the nineteenth and twentieth centuries. He revolutionized science fiction while

Queen Victoria still reigned and then lived to comment on the destruction of Hiroshima. As Europe slid into its ghastly years of trench warfare in 1914, he published *The World Set Free*, a futuristic novel imagining—with unintended irony, as he later realized—utopian consequences of atomic bombs as instigators of a world government that would liberate humanity from the specter of warring nation-states. In 1901 he invented modern futurology as an art of rational, not religious, forecast, though without giving it this dismal name, in *Anticipations of the Reaction of Mechanical and Scientific Progress upon Human Life and Thought*. His masterpieces had appeared by the turn of the century: *The Time Machine* in 1895 and *The War of the Worlds* in 1898. Other notable works of his early years are *The Island of Doctor Moreau* (1896); *The Invisible Man* (1897); *When the Sleeper Wakes* (1899); *The First Men in the Moon* (1901); *The Food of the Gods* (1904); *A Modern Utopia* (1905); *In The Days of the Comet* (1906); and *The War in the Air* (1908). Along with many short stories in and outside the boundaries of science fiction Wells also published his best realistic novels during the amazingly varied outset of his career: *Love and Mr. Lewisham* (1900); *Kipps* (1905); *Tono-Bungay* (1909); *Ann Veronica* (1909); and *The History of Mr. Polly* (1910). If all these books are ideologically consistent in depicting civilization's discontents in ways that implicitly or explicitly strengthen the case for that New Republic of technocrats that Wells proposes in *Anticipations* and dramatizes in *A Modern Utopia*, their very diverse forms could hardly be pursued with equal energy over the next thirty-six years. Wells turned not only from what he called scientific romance but also increasingly away from fiction itself to advocacy of a rational world state. He tried to make reality conform to a science fiction writer's visions by polemic concentration on autobiography, essays, and didactic history. Consequently Wells as public figure overshadowed for a while the works that had initially gained him an audience. His career prefigures the tendency of twentieth-century science fiction to spill outside of its boundaries as a literary genre.

With cruel accuracy, George Orwell judged the later Wells "too sane to understand the modern world" in which "nationalism, religious bigotry and feudal loyalty are far more powerful forces than what he himself would describe as sanity." Orwell also acknowledged the astuteness of Wells as prophet before

1914 and the power of his imaginative vision for those who grew up reading his scientific romances: "The minds of all of us, and therefore the physical world, would be perceptibly different if Wells had never existed. . . . There you were, in a world of pedants, clergymen and golfers, with your future employers exhorting you to 'get on or get out,' your parents systematically warping your sexual life, and your dull-witted schoolmasters sniggering over their Latin tags; and here was this wonderful man who could tell you about the inhabitants of the planets and the bottom of the sea, and who *knew* that the future was not going to be what respectable people imagined."[13] The inevitability of surprising change is thus the message that perceptive readers like Orwell found underlying the ideological complexities of Wells's fiction. Its distinction was less in its prophecies than in its invitation to see life in ways unimagined by "respectable people." Wells offered a counterculture. Indeed his best scientific romances are hardly concerned with prediction in any specific sense. Their purpose is not to alert us to the imminence of time travel, Martian invasion, wonderful comet strikes, invisible men, discovery of strange creatures on the moon, surgical alteration of animals to resemble humans, or invention of food that will create a race of giants. Wells employs such more or less—usually less—scientifically explained phenomena as a basis for looking at the present from new angles of vision.

"An ingenious use of scientific patter" is Wells's own rather too dismissive description of his technique in the scientific romances throughout which, he insisted, his "early, profound and lifelong admiration for Swift, appears again and again . . . and . . . is particularly evident in a predisposition to make the stories reflect upon contemporary political and social discussions."[14] Wells's social commentary is most conspicuously Swiftian in his opposition of big and little people in *The Food of the Gods*, and in recurring variations of Houyhnhnms and Yahoos apparent in the Eloi and Morlocks found by the Time Traveller, the beast-people created by Dr. Moreau, and the elaborately rational Selenite society that Cavor and Bedford discover on the moon. A truly Swiftian savage indignation animates such moments of biting satire as the reactionary's resistance to the new scientifically invented nutrient Herakleophorbia, the "food of the Gods" that turns ordinary people into giants: "No one . . .

wishes to prevent the children of the lower classes obtaining an education suited to their condition, but to give them a food of this sort will be to destroy their sense of proportion utterly. . . . What Good will it do, he asks, to make poor people six-and-thirty feet high?"[15] What good indeed. *The Time Machine*'s cannibalistic Morlocks living underground to tend machinery, descendants of the working classes preying on the aboveground Eloi who trace their ancestry to the ruling classes, are in clear dialogic relationship to *A Modest Proposal*. Just as Swift there brings to disturbing life the metaphor of rich people devouring the poor, so in *The Time Machine* Wells vividly dramatizes the alarming corollary that in return poor people will eventually rise up and devour the rich. Every attentive reader of Swift and Wells can multiply such instances of adroit variation on Swiftian themes and tropes.

It is only partly because of such affinities, however, that Darko Suvin can argue that "the clearest paradigm of SF is to be found in *Gulliver's Travels*, and that Wells closely followed it" in *The Time Machine*, although "substituting Darwinist evolution for Swiftian or Christian-humanist ethics." For Suvin the distinctive touch that carries Wells beyond mere imitation of Swift is transformation of science into art: "*The principle of a Wellsian structure of science fiction is mutation of scientific into aesthetic cognition.*"[16] Thus regarded, the scientific component is more than mere patter. Conversely, the aesthetic transformation of science is more than mere sugar-coating on a didactic pill as it so often (but deceptively) seems to be in Verne. And as Wells suggested in affiliating himself not only to Swift but to *Frankenstein*, Lucian, *The Golden Ass of Apuleius* (second century A.D.), *Peter Schlemihl* (1814), and even David Garnett's *Lady into Fox* (1922), the artistry of Wellsian scientific romance at its best centers less on the prominence of social commentary than on the varied perspectives from which readers are invited to perceive the aesthetic possibilities of a scientific hypothesis.

The tales vary considerably, however, in their actual concern with science. Some are Swiftian fantasy in which the scientific component is negligible. In Wells's most powerful short story, "The Country of the Blind," for example, first published in 1904 in the *Strand Magazine*, there is neither credibility nor scientific interest in the premise of an isolated Ecuadorian valley populat-

ed for fifteen generations by blind descendants of original set-
tlers victimized by a strange disease that not only deprived them
of sight but rendered them transmitters of blindness. Their situation is merely a convenient basis for stinging satire whose vehicle
is the blind people's hostility to a sighted man who arrives and,
far from becoming king, is ostracized for presuming to inform
them about things that he alone can see. They will accept him
only if he agrees to have his eyes put out and become blind like
them. As an allegory of the difficulties created by people's indifference to what they themselves cannot experience, "The
Country of the Blind" dramatizes a predicament often enough
faced by scientists, but also by intellectuals and visionaries of all
kinds. The dubious scientific premise of genetically transmitted
blindness to which a whole village has adapted serves only as a
means of establishing opposed viewpoints—of the sighted man
versus the blind populace—whose clash generates the story's
considerable dramatic interest as well as its meanings.

So too for the unconvincing explanations of invisibility in *The
Invisible Man*. Hilarious slapstick comedy and then thought-pro-
voking satire are facilitated by resort to vague ideas about optics
that are of little significance even where scientifically accurate,
but that allow for opposition between the perspectives of an
invisible man and those upon whom he acts unseen. Here the
scientist who has become invisible and thereby alienated himself
from humanity does so for selfish purposes that make him an
unsympathetic figure in the line of Frankenstein and Moreau.
The savage hatred directed at him by ordinary visible people,
however, makes it hard to approve of their eagerness to destroy
what they cannot comprehend. Like sight in the land of the
blind, invisibility is more effective as symbol than as science.

In the Days of the Comet offers the least credible of Wells's scientific premises by resorting to a comet strike covering the earth
with a gas that eliminates everybody's murderous and destructive impulses, thus leading to peace, prosperity, and free love for
all. Despite the absurdity of this device, the first part of *In the
Days of the Comet* is a gripping autobiographical account of a man
driven to the brink of murder because of what he takes to be
social injustices. The second part is a sketchy utopia that can be
judged successful only if measured by the controversy that its
advocacy of free love stirred up upon publication. The main

structural device of this novel is contrast between the outlooks of pre- and postutopian days, a contrast sustained by the technique of a retrospective narrator telling of his murderous younger self from the vantage point of someone writing for a utopian audience who will find incredible the social inequities and hardships taken for granted in *our* (pre-comet) time. This is the most hybrid of Wells's scientific romances in its attempt to mingle utopia with social realism, and it therefore illustrates all the more clearly how he tends to introduce a scientific premise not primarily for evaluation as a hypothesis or as a basis for prediction but to create new perspectives from which to defamiliarize the reader's world.

In *The Food of the Gods* a synthetic nutrient that stimulates growth symbolizes the enabling power of science to revolutionize social relationships. The narrative derives its force, however, not from presenting an aesthetic correlative for the actual possibility of such a stimulant or any other product of biochemistry, but from Wells's Swiftian skill at turning a realistic account of clashes between big people and little people into an allegory of conflict between haves and have-nots, and between new possibilities for a better future represented by the big people and conservative resistance to change exemplified in the small—and petty-minded—politicians who oppose creating a race of giants that will supersede them. *The Food of the Gods* pays homage to Lilliput and Brobdingnag by echoing the clashing perspectives of these strange places while locating their conflicting viewpoints right at home, outside the reader's window.

The Island of Doctor Moreau is an elegant variation on *Frankenstein* focusing less on the scientist's capacity to unleash trouble than on his resemblance to God. Dr. Moreau's beast-people do not escape from his island to spread terror. But neither does he succeed in his God-like attempt to fashion them after his own—our own—human image. Even if they are taken as referring to evolution's blind alleys (perhaps including ourselves), and thus as a glance at Darwinian versions of creation, their regression to yahoolike bestiality is for readers less a transformation of scientific into aesthetic cognition than a disturbing theological allegory suggesting both human incapacity for attaining an ethical existence and God's inability to carry out his purposes. Where Victor Frankenstein is indicted for irresponsibility toward a creature that has been fashioned all too efficiently, Dr. Moreau is guilty of incompetence along with deliberate indifference to the pain he inflicts while trying to perfect his creative methods. He is a bumbling god indifferent to suffering who does not know how to make higher creatures from lower ones. He cannot make evolution work. His experiments fail. It is no wonder that Wells regarded *The Island of Doctor Moreau* in its 1896 context chiefly as an exercise in youthful blasphemy. Viewed now, Moreau's horrible closed society controlled from above by scientifically inflicted pain is more likely to seem, as it does to Frank McConnell, "perhaps the first really totalitarian regime imagined by Western man." McConnell is right to add that "Wells is never more brilliant than in understanding the connection between romantic aspiration and tawdry, bestial, murderous practice that underlies so many twentieth-century totalitarianisms."[17] As an anti-utopia presenting an island with a society worse than the reader's, less human and more inhumane, *The Island of Doctor Moreau* thus prefigures Orwell's more explicit insight into the sinister connections possible between science and government. But it is political more than scientific cognitions for which both *Nineteen Eighty-Four* and *The Island of Doctor Moreau* find suitable aesthetic correlatives.

Even *The War of the Worlds* depends more on political than scientific premises for its power. The idea of ugly hostile aliens from outer space stems, it is true, from a long tradition of scientific speculation about the possibility of life on other worlds.[18] Certainly, too, the notion of technologically superior invaders arriving on spaceships could only be given such effective shape in the nineteenth-century (or later) context of a scientifically advanced society with formidable high-tech weaponry of its own as well as a sophisticated astronomy much concerned with our neighboring planets. Mars especially became a focus of scientific and popular attention thanks to Percival Lowell's obsession with what he took to be artificial canals on its surface. The title of his 1908 book *Mars as the Abode of Life* sums up the hypothesis to which he gave credibility and wide publicity in a series of popular studies starting with *Mars* in 1895, three years before Wells published *The War of the Worlds*. But granting that context, and given too Wells's talent for making even the most unlikely tale read like fact, what animates *The War of the Worlds* is use of a scientific premise—the possibility of an encounter with a more technologically advanced extraterrestrial civilization—to create a fundamental shift in political perspective whereby readers are shown what it is like to be on the receiving end of an imperial enterprise. We are made to see for a change how it would feel if they did it to us.

Wells raises the political stakes of Chesney's variety of future-war story by suggesting that all humanity, not just England, is at risk. Early in the narrative, however, any self-righteous impulse to condemn the Martians is countered by reminders of European wars of extermination waged against Tasmanian and other natives: "Are we such apostles of mercy as to complain if the Martians warred in the same spirit?" Readers are later invited to an even greater imaginative leap after a grisly account of Martians nourishing themselves with blood taken from living humans: "The bare idea of this is no doubt horribly repulsive to us, but at the same time I think that we should remember how repulsive our carnivorous habits would seem to an intelligent rabbit."[19] To put ourselves in the position of natives our culture has displaced or destroyed, much less to think of ourselves as intelligent rabbits (a nice Swiftian conceit), is a far different exercise from considering the validity or consequences of some purely scientific hypothesis.

Throughout *The War of the Worlds*, Wells includes invitations to perceive from multiple viewpoints both its action and what that action symbolizes. Some of these shifts work primarily to augment narrative verisimilitude by presenting action in a kind of depth not attainable from only one angle of vision. In describing how people flee in terror from the Martian war machines ravaging London and the English countryside, for example, Wells recounts population displacements that symbolize those inflicted by Europeans on others in the past while eerily prefiguring the recurring flight of refugees that was to be a sadly characteristic feature of the twentieth century. He also invites readers to imagine such scenes both as experienced by participants and as they would appear to a detached observer floating overhead in a balloon. We are now so used to aerial shots of disaster scenes that it may require a moment's reflection to appreciate how skillfully Wells employs the technology of flight circa 1898 to vary perspectives on the events of his story, and thus on the real world about which it is a metaphoric commentary. In this way too, concern with technology is subordinated to artistry. The scientifically plausible framework of encounter with technologically superior aliens is indispensable to *The War of the Worlds* and the subgenre of science fiction for which it is the archetype. But of equal importance for Wells is subordination of such frameworks to aesthetic effects in the service of better purposes than Gothic horror for its own sake, prediction of future technology, or (as too many of his imitators prefer) cultivation of xenophobia.

The First Men in the Moon, which starts with an epigram from "Lucien's *Icaromenippus*," is explicitly in the Lucianic tradition of lunar voyages. But its well-organized Selenites are even more closely affiliated with Swift's Houyhnhnms. Neither set of aliens represents the translation of a scientific premise into an aesthetic cognition. They derive from the realms of utopian fantasy. Here the contrast with Verne's moon voyages goes beyond his shaky claim to greater plausibility for his giant cannon than Wells could muster for Cavor's invention of a metal alloy with antigravity properties. The crucial difference is Verne's preoccupation with the facts—known and extrapolated—of space travel and lunar geography as opposed to Wells's use of travel to the moon primarily as a device allowing for invention of a beautiful though menacing landscape along with a society more disconcerting in its ant-heap rationality than the Houyhnhnms but without equal claims to moral superiority. From that perspective readers are invited to reconsider the haphazard social arrangements of their own world. But there is little concern with science.

In *The Time Machine*, explanations of the time machine itself may be dismissed as scientific patter at its most obfuscating: such devices are impossible. As a literary convention initiated by Wells and indispensable to later science fiction, however, the time machine deserves high praise: first because it is presented as a *machine*, not some kind of time-traveling enchantment. This keeps the tale and its readers within the cognitive boundaries of science, not magic, because we are accustomed to machinery of all kinds that we do not really understand but assume is operating on some rational principle derived from science. Second and of equal importance, the time machine serves as a means of conveying us imaginatively to otherwise unattainable situations that are connected in one way or another with real science, not pseudophysics. It also allows a return voyage to provide readers with memories of a future that may shape present attitudes.

At the Time Traveller's first destination in A.D. 802,701 the divergence of humanity into Eloi and Morlocks interrogates Darwinian theories about the evolution of species by presenting a situation that seems more like a case of reverse evolution toward lesser intelligence and, for the unfortunate Eloi especially, lesser adaptability. Wells poses for readers the problem of whether civilization may short-circuit the process by which, according to Darwin, nature ensures adaptation to changing environments. We are confronted with the issue of how society and evolution are related. At the Time Traveller's final destination more than thirty million years in the future, sublime scenes of a dying planet and expiring sun dramatize cosmological theories about our solar system's ultimate fate. Through the Time Traveller's eyes we can see what those theories imply not only for present philosophy but for human experience—or more precisely, what those theories would imply if there could be any such thing as human experience of our world's last moments. Above all, *The Time Machine* drives home emotional as well as philosophical understanding of what geology from Buffon forward had discovered about the sheer vastness of geological time. More relentlessly but also more beautifully in its tragic mode than any other work of Western literature, *The Time Machine* confronts us with the shattering implications of time's inhuman duration.

En route to the eclipse experienced on that beach which is journey's end for life on our planet as well as for the Time Traveller—and the archetype for so many terminal beaches in science fiction that pay tribute to the power of Wells's apocalyptic vision—the Time Traveller is compelled to reconsider his assumptions about progress.[20] When he stops among the Eloi, their country at first strikes him as altogether utopian by virtue of its apparently happy people leading what seems a carefree life in the sunshine amid pastoral landscapes. But unlike conventional literary utopias, there is no guide. Instead there is a puzzling statue of the Sphinx whose enigmatic presence and sinister role as a place where Morlocks conceal the time machine suggest a mythic dimension in which the Time Traveller symbolically becomes a latter-day Oedipus trying to solve a riddle of unknown import. Only very gradually by a process of hypothesis formation that mimics the scientific method—while achieving too the structure of a classic detective story—does the Time Traveller piece together the disturbing truth about human devolution to the Morlocks' cannibalism and the Eloi's mental vacuity, both signaling civilization's collapse.

The circle has come round, the Time Traveller concludes, from cannibal ancestors to cannibal descendants. Weena's devotion, strikingly though sentimentally symbolized by the flowers from her that he brings back to the nineteenth century, is the only remaining vestige of common humanity. He finds that nineteenth-century ideas of progress were wrong. In humanity's future, regress prevails. Utopia has come and gone. It could not cope with change. Its temporary achievement was of no significance. He speculates that biological division into Eloi and Morlocks was the result of social segregation imposed between rulers and workers. As a theory about a past (which is for readers the future) this may seem more parody than application of Darwinian ideas about divergence of species. What the Time Traveller encounters, however, becomes for readers not primarily a thought experiment testing the validity of Darwin's evolutionary theories but rather a metaphorical application of those theories to depict a situation designed to caution against the dangers as well as the inhumanity of rigidly dividing our own society into rich and poor.

What makes this warning more than an ineffectual abstraction is Wells's great narrative power in depicting by gradual increments the horrifying appearance and habits of the Morlocks along with the increasing terror aroused in the Time Traveller— with whom readers identify—by his dangerous encounters with them. Because it is the inequities of our society that have created these future monsters, we find *ourselves*—not some mad scientist whom it is easy to detest and forget—accused of playing the role of Victor Frankenstein. By acquiescence in the status quo we are making monsters. In Wells's stunningly original variation of Mary Shelley's theme it is we who are the dangerous counterparts of Frankenstein, while the Time Traveller as representative scientist plays the more noble role of a modern Oedipus trying to solve the ultimate riddle of human destiny.

The Palace of Green Porcelain episode is another tour-de-force in suggestive narration and variation of viewpoint. As the Time Traveller wanders with the devoted but uncomprehending

Weena through this vast museum, "some latter-day South Kensington" that sums up in its exhibits the entire history of the human race and indeed of life on our planet, what stands out is how little is actually described. Many (but how many?) rooms full of machinery, animal remains, and cultural artifacts are mentioned vaguely. Of future weapons we are told only about guns made "of some new metal."[21] In another gallery there is "a vast array of idols—Polynesian, Mexican, Grecian, Phoenician, every country on earth" (*TM*, 86). The rise and fall of innumerable civilizations and their technologies is thus implied but left for readers to picture in detail if they can. In this way Wells involves us imaginatively. What he took to be a defect of futuristic fiction— its need for readers to help out the author—is in the practice of a masterpiece like *The Time Machine* actually a great strength. Here and elsewhere in this magnificently concise work Wells successfully follows the classical prescription for attaining the sublime: by hints and omissions that suggest awe-inspiring vistas—temporal more than spatial in this case—rather than by providing those myriad details that make everything seem commonplace. The point, after all, of our vicarious visit to the Palace of Green Porcelain is that we are *not* at our South Kensington but more than 800,000 years away.

At that remove the Time Traveller muses on the futility of literature (including scientific records) while standing in a library of which there remains only "the decaying vestiges of books" that strike him as a "sombre wilderness of rotting paper" (*TM*, 84). He thinks ruefully of his own now-vanished seventeen articles on optics. We may think about all those (to us) future inventions exhibited to no ultimate purpose in the Palace of Green Porcelain alongside equally decaying and forgotten relics of our present and past. Ironically this view backward from a remote future does not tell us anything about our own immediate future, which is thus in a peculiar sense forgotten before it takes place.[22] The Time Traveller's tour of this museum invites us to consider our present and future as a lost past that finally has not mattered.

Of all the artifacts in the Palace of Green Porcelain the Time Traveller only takes away matches, camphor, and a metal bar that can serve as both club and lever. Fire, weapon, and tool become the emblems of civilization. With fire he staves off the

Morlocks, whose eyes cannot stand bright illumination after centuries of adaptation to a subterranean existence. But his control of fire is imperfect. The Morlocks take Weena when the campfire goes out as he dozes off. He also accidentally starts a forest fire that creates a post-Darwinian version of Hell: a "weird and horrible" scene of apocalyptic chaos as blinded Morlocks, described as "these damned souls," stumble away from and sometimes into the flames while the Time Traveller beats off those who get too close to him. He is a genius who cannot keep a campfire going and takes a primitive solace in bashing his enemies, momentarily enjoying "the strange exultation that so often seems to accompany hard fighting" (*TM*, 92–95). As he finally mounts the time machine for his escape, it is not fire but brute force that allows him to shake off the Morlocks' last attempt to grab him. Despite the ingenuity of his time machine, a device symbolizing the technological reach of our civilization, the Time Traveller's failures suggest that he represents a culture unable fully to control either its resources or its ultimate destiny.

Throughout *The Time Machine*, Wells avoids the temptation to invent fancy futuristic gadgetry or even describe complicated technology of his own day. Instead he resorts to devices that sustain symbolic oppositions between light and darkness, above ground and underground, privileged and oppressed. The Time Traveller does not bring along from the nineteenth century a rifle, revolver, or even camping equipment. Nor does he take away from the Palace of Green Porcelain any of its advanced weapons or even a sword. By sticking to basics such as matches and levers, Wells achieves a powerful symbolism that is not weakened by reference to the real or imagined shapes of machinery that will inevitably seem dated after a few years, the fate of so much lesser science fiction whose spaceships, ray guns, and other hardware soon acquire a quaint period air of failed extrapolation or outmoded novelty that distracts from the story.

The Time Traveller twice experiences "a deadly nausea": once while escaping from his underground encounter with the Morlocks, and again during the eclipse that marks the terminus of his journey and of life on earth. It is "a horror of this great darkness" that ushers in the second attack (*TM*, 106). As it was to be in Jean-Paul Sartre's novel of that title, nausea in *The Time Machine* is symbolic of the human predicament in a meaningless universe. Morlocks and Eloi are in their different ways equally shocking deviations from the continuing upward spiral of evolution implicit in post-Darwinian theories of progress. So is the horrifying series of even more primitive creatures found by the Time Traveller at his final stops. As in those unforgettable descriptions of Martians and their towering machines in *The War of the Worlds*, Wells creates archetypes for science fiction's most threatening aliens. But in *The Time Machine* those aliens are our descendants. It is earth itself that produces the final alien invasion: they come from here. They win. Wells populates our remote future first with the decayed remnants of human form, then with menacing crablike monstrosities of gigantic size, and finally with an unnerving little "thing" about the size of a football "hopping fitfully about" with tentacles (how many?) trailing down from it "black against the weltering blood-red water" (*TM*, 106). Existential nausea is the only possible response to this spectacle in its setting of "that remote and awful twilight" (*TM*, 106).

As in *Frankenstein*, a framing narrative includes self-reflexive comments on the tale and its meaning: setting aside the question of credibility and "taking it as a story, what do you think of it?" the Time Traveller asks his friends (*TM*, 109). Without answering that question, the unnamed reporter of the Time Traveller's narration, Wells's equivalent of Walton though of far less dramatic importance, offers in the epilogue an existential resolution of the dilemma posed by the impending extinction of humanity: "If that is so, it remains for us to live as though it were not so" (*TM*, 114). Readers are thus offered at least a philosophical modus vivendi, however unsatisfying, for coping with the tale's implications. To judge it as a story we are, wisely, left to our own conclusions. The verdict has been favorable. This is Wells at his best and science fiction at its best. The era of Eloi and Morlocks is surely the most compelling anti-utopia before *Nineteen Eighty-Four*. The final glimpses of a dying planet are at once among the most sublime vistas in English literature and unsurpassed in their achievement of a powerfully affecting aesthetic correlative for that entropy which according to science may well be the inescapable destiny of our universe and is certainly the fate of each individual. To recurring imagery of darkness culminating in the eclipse, Wells memorably joins allusions to a great silence: "All the sounds of man, the bleating of sheep, the cries of birds, the hum of insects, the stir that makes the background of our lives—all that was over. . . . I saw the black central shadow of the eclipse sweeping towards me. In another moment the pale stars alone were visible. All else was rayless obscurity. The sky was absolutely black" (*TM*, 106). Here even more explicitly than in the Arctic landscapes of *Frankenstein* a scene on earth takes us to the edge of space where we confront our relationship to the stars. But Wells also takes us to the brink of a temporal gulf that is equally ominous. *The Time Machine* brings home to earth the silence of infinite space and joins to its Pascalian terrors our dread of infinite time.

3

France: Technophilia

Cogito, ergo sum.
> René Descartes

He is a true Frenchman, ballasted on one side by a treatise on the integral and differential calculus, and on the other by a voyage around the globe.
> Denis Diderot, *Supplement to Bougainville's "Voyage"*

You are going to travel in the land of marvels.
> Captain Nemo

Before Verne: From Guttin to Geoffroy

Pourquoi j'ai tué Jules Verne (Why I killed Jules Verne), Bernard Blanc's 1978 book on contemporary French science fiction, opens with an account of how the author, bizarrely disguised in a 1970s punk outfit, goes back to 1905 and kills Verne in the study of his home at Amiens by plying him with sugar to induce a fatal diabetes attack after first stabbing his wife Honorine lest she survive to write memoirs glorifying his memory.[1] Before polishing Verne off Blanc bitterly reproaches him (as they chat over drinks) for those rockets and submarines that created a corrupt taste for such things among youth and led his successors to spend the next fifty years off in space pillaging the planets. Unlike his chum Wells, Blanc also complains, Verne was not even a socialist: his spaceships belong to rich people. Noticing a model of the *Nautilus* on the mantelpiece Blanc furiously throws his empty glass at it but misses. Verne is mortal but the products of his imagination are untouchable. Blanc does not explain why he picked the year of Verne's actual death instead of sending himself or some other frustrated French science fiction writer from the twentieth century to murder Verne before his debut in 1863 with *Five Weeks in a Balloon*, thus eliminating at once Verne's oeuvre and his influence. Blanc's point is that French science fiction is unimaginable without Verne although stifled by his fascination with technology.

Only by a symbolic killing of their father, Blanc suggests, can Verne's literary children achieve their own identity: nothing useful can now be done in his way. Blanc's polemic is of course unfair to Verne as well as to the diversity of subsequent French science fiction. During the decade after France's domestic troubles of 1968, Anglophone New Wave science fiction and the French New Novel along with other stirrings of postmodernism had accelerated a long-standing preoccupation with psychological and social rather than more narrowly technological topics. Blanc was actually writing in the midst of that shift in France toward concern with ecology and psychology signaled most famously by Jean-Pierre Andrevon's science fiction anthologies entitled *Return to the Earth*. Andrevon laments not Verne, but post–World War II American influences that alienated French science fiction from its true roots, which he traces back to Jules Verne.[2] Nevertheless *Why I Killed Jules Verne* does reveal the extent to which even amid a massive rejection of Vernian narrative models his wonderful machines still defined the expectations brought to science fiction by French readers and writers.

Equally paradoxical is Verne's relationship to his predecessors and contemporaries. Despite a strain of technophilia that I shall stress here because it is ultimately of great significance for the genre, the majority of French science fiction and its prototypes from Cyrano de Bergerac to the eve of World War I is either indifferent or hostile to technology. Verne wrote amid increasing

skepticism that technological progress heralds utopia. Nevertheless it is Vernian technophilia that prevailed. It prevailed over his
rivals, who sank into obscurity while he achieved worldwide
fame. It even prevailed over his own doubts that inclined him to
write sequels in which he finally destroys such menacing
machinery as Nemo's submarine and Robur's airships while cau-
tioning against the megalomaniacal uses to which they might all
too easily be put. But he could no more eliminate a favorable
view of them from public imagination than Arthur Conan Doyle
could get rid of Sherlock Holmes. Although in the latter phase of
his career Verne himself was increasingly alert to industrial technology's destructive side, his work indelibly established the marvelous machine as one of science fiction's archetypal tropes.
Despite the sinister potentialities of submarine and aerial warfare
foreshadowed by Nemo's *Nautilus* and Robur's *Albatros* and
Epouvante, and despite too the vividly dramatized cannon and
poison gas shells of the evil Stahlstadt (Steel City) established by
the mad scientist Schultz in *Les Cinq Cents Millions de la Bégum*
(*The Bégum's Fortune*, 1879), Verne's submarines, aircraft, and
spaceships are mostly remembered as utopian vehicles of liberation, not instruments of apocalypse. Verne's most enduring legacy is a collective imagination of the beneficent machine.

Another paradox of Verne's relationship to other French writers is his rejection of the future as a locus of narration. It was,
after all, his compatriot Félix Bodin's 1834 manifesto *Le Roman de
l'avenir* that first proposed the quintessential Vernian topics of
aerial and submarine voyages while specifying that only fully
realized future settings would allow such material enough
verisimilitude to work as an effective replacement for outmoded
epic marvels and thus create a true *littérature futuriste* retaining
the appeal of fantasy but discarding reliance on the supernatural.
All Verne's major works, however, are set in the present or in the
immediate past with respect to their dates of publication. Verne
makes futuristic devices such as the *Nautilus* part of his contemporary world rather than taking readers forward imaginatively
to a very different future where such things are commonplace. In
effect he imports from the future a few items of advanced technology, usually one at a time and under guise of a prior invention: something constructed (secretly) a few years ago rather
than a breakthrough to be achieved many years hence. Travel

through space rather than time is his specialty. With him readers explore on land, under water, and in the air. They journey to the center of the earth. They travel around the moon and back. But they do not tour the future.

This preference has been variously explained as a concern with imaginatively portraying those watershed moments where the present interacts with the future, as a conservative reluctance to present science as an agent of disruptive change, and as a device for establishing a new mythology of lost origins that allows radical technological advance to be assimilated as continuity.[3] Thus regarded, Verne's conceit that such things as a trip around the moon or a prolonged submarine or aerial voyage have *already* taken place not only gives science fiction its social role—even more important now—of preventing future shock by allowing easier psychological accommodation to corresponding realities when they materialize. It also replicates at a mythic level the widespread nineteenth-century scientific assumption, prominent in such texts as Darwin's *Origin of Species* and later in Freudian case histories, that for everything it is possible to find or at least hypothesize starting points that have always existed even if they have hitherto remained unknown. Certainly too, as H. G. Wells was to remark, novelistic verisimilitude could more easily be achieved by resort to the familiar details of past and present life for background.[4] In temporal settings, though not in the devices around which his plots revolve, Verne responded to the pressure for conformity created by the success of realistic novels. But whatever the explanation for his avoidance of overt engagement with the future, Verne's disinclination to set stories ahead in time is remarkably at variance with the French tradition of pioneering in this dimension.

To France belongs the distinction of publishing in 1659, long before Bodin articulated an aesthetics of futuristic fiction, the first book of secular fiction actually set in future time: Jacques Guttin's *Epigone, histoire du siècle futur* (Epigone, a story of the future century). Despite its originality of concept, Guttin lacked the ability or nerve to carry this incomplete romance beyond a tentatively realized experiment in which the depicted future hardly differs from exotic contemporary or past settings of similar romances offering little food for thought and much high adventure in remote lands. *Epigone* was soon forgotten.[5] It was also in France, however, that a tale of the future first achieved significant impact with publication in 1771 of Louis-Sébastien Mercier's *L'An 2440* (The year 2440).

Its narrator dreams of sleeping 700 years to awake in a twenty-fifth-century Paris where the Bastille has been demolished and despotism replaced by a benevolent government presiding over a beautiful city whose enlightened inhabitants have long been free from tyranny and superstition. Mercier's point in contrasting this utopian future with life under Louis XV was so clear that *L'An 2440* was banned in France, put on the Inquisition's list of forbidden books in 1773—and very widely read throughout Europe during the rest of the eighteenth century in eleven French editions along with two English translations and translations into Dutch, Italian, and German. It was the first utopia printed in North America (Washington and Jefferson owned copies). It was an underground best-seller inside France before the Revolution. Afterward Mercier claimed to have been its prophet. His vision of a twenty-fifth-century Paris free alike from repressive government and its detested symbol the Bastille actually functioned not as forecast but as encouragement of those changes that began in 1789. For Mercier, as for so many others in the eighteenth century, the crucial transformations are political, not scientific. Technology is not an issue in *L'An 2440*. Nor was the incipient industrial revolution in any apparent way a stimulus to Mercier's imagination of the future.[6] Enlightenment ideals of freedom and tolerance eloquently expressed in *L'An 2440*, moreover, were less innovative and ultimately less influential than its future setting. This became the pattern for a new genre.

Mercier was the first to adopt a specific future date as the entire title for a work of fiction, thus paving the way for efforts culminating in Orwell's masterful use of this device. Even more crucially for the history of literary forms, *L'An 2440* is the first utopia set in future time. Mercier thus inaugurated the shift from utopia, the good place that is also no place, to uchronia: the good future time. Because *L'An 2440* shows a better future in a real location—Paris—rather than portraying, as Sir Thomas More and his imitators did, an ideal society on an imaginary island, Mercier connected utopia to history by offering a vision of potential change set ahead in time but explicitly proposed as a possibility for the reader's own world: a desirable and perhaps realizable terminus for actual history. Displacement of utopia from the imaginary island to the real place in future time is in formal importance second only to More's publication of *Utopia*. Arguably too, the genre More created was perfected by translation of utopian settings to the future because only by a connection with history can utopias offer much prospect of influence in the real world. Dreams like Mercier's of a better future and Orwellian nightmares of a worse one may evoke political action, or at least political awareness, of a kind unlikely to be aroused merely by imagining an island whose charms or horrors have no temporal link to that history which shapes readers' lives, and which they may in turn help to shape. Perhaps it was knowledge of Mercier's connection with the French Revolution, or merely intuition of futuristic fiction's great potential for encouraging disruptive political change, that made Verne wary of setting his novels in the future.

Following the upheavals of 1789 and their aftermath, in any case, futuristic fiction gathered momentum with France again in the lead. Nicolas-Edme Restif de la Bretonne was the first to exploit a very far future setting, although without complete success, in *Les Posthumes* (The posthumous, 1802). This portrays several million years of future history within the complicated frame-narrative of a story supposedly written by the Illuminist author Jacques Cazotte, who was guillotined during the Terror in 1792. Restif sketches biological evolution amid vast geological changes, including the appearance of a second moon, as a backdrop for the life of Duke Multipliandre, a man born in the eighteenth century with the ability to project his mind into the bodies of other people and thus survive through succeeding eras to witness drastic social transformations along with radical mutations of the human form. At the end of this sprawling fantasy of immortality and evolution the story loops back to describe Multipliandre's horrifying encounters with violence during the French Revolution, a theme recalling the actual fate of *Les Posthumes'* putative author Cazotte and many others. Here too, technology is not an issue. Restif's scientific speculation centers on biology and geology extrapolated without much constraint by known facts but with a shrewd intuition of possible changes implied by eighteenth-century hypotheses about the vastness of planetary time scales. The significance of *Les Posthumes* as a major step toward effective forms of futuristic science fiction lies not in such extrapolation but in Restif's creation of a narrative structure inviting readers to view a specific historical event of their own recent past, the French Revolution, from the estranging perspective of an imaginary future.

Except for decorative purposes in the form of exotic airships, technology is equally irrelevant to human fate in Jean-Baptiste Cousin de Grainville's *Le dernier homme* (1805), translated into English in 1806 as *The Last Man; or, Omegarus and Syderia, A Romance in Futurity*. Here we find the first of those many last men who populate science fiction. Grainville's *The Last Man* inaugurates a genre of stories recounting the end of human history.[7] His narrative is a daring but not altogether compatible or coherently dialogic mixture of modes. It unevenly combines epic, biblical, and novelistic features to portray apocalypse in an undated far future that is presented as mythic rather than historical or geological time. Grainville's doomed lovers Omegarus and Syderia, earth's last fertile couple, must contend with a dying planet marked by exhaustion of natural resources, depopulation, and reversion of humanity's remnants to savagery amid the ruins of once-great cities. God sends Adam back to earth to persuade them not to have children so that time will end, the final judgment will take place, and eternity begin. Earth's Guardian Spirit tries to prevent this outcome but fails. The conclusion is a vivid account of how Omegarus, Syderia, and a few others living through the last days experience the ensuing cataclysm along with curious problems posed by simultaneous resurrection of all the earth's dead. Grainville's *The Last Man* is most successful as a stimulus to more coherent variations of its theme by later writers, and as a partial secularization of Apocalypse that embeds within its prevailing allegory and fantasy a realistic depiction of the tempo of human experience during a collective crisis. Although partly inspired by *Le dernier homme* as well as Defoe's *Robinson Crusoe* and *A Journal of the Plague Year*, Mary Shelley's *The Last Man* (1826) proved a more viable model for science fiction's versions of apocalypse because it was more thoroughly secularized. But in it she too avoids engagement with questions about technology by resorting to the arbitrary device of a plague rather than machinery of any kind or even scientific meddling with biology à la Frankenstein as the agent of humanity's final catastrophe.

Technology first dominates the future in Emile Souvestre's *Le Monde tel qu'il sera* (The world as it will be, 1846). Its method is satire. Its purpose is to warn against industrialization that could bring into existence a "world where man had become enslaved by machines and where interest had replaced love."[8] This bleak future is witnessed by Souvestre's nineteenth-century protagonists Martha and Maurice, whose curiosity about where the tendencies of their epoch will lead is satisfied when its guardian spirit, John Progress, materializes outside their garret on his flying steam locomotive (and dressed like a banker) to grant their wish by putting them into a mesmeric trance from which they awaken in the year 3000. They are dismayed to find a world that includes among its progressive horrors steam-machines for raising children in "colleges" from birth until age eighteen; physicians who diagnose *everyone* as mentally ill; bridges replaced by giant cannon firing people across rivers in huge cannonballs fitted out with seats and windows for passengers; underground railroads; writing machines for commercially producing different genres at top speed; a "perpetual newspaper" printed on an endless sheet of paper that flows through each house on a conveyor belt; a feminist named Mlle Spartacus who sells subscriptions for printing in ninety-two volumes her works, "the world's revolution in manuscript"; a republic ruled by an empty armchair (known as "l'impeccable"); and an enterprising capitalist who has purchased Switzerland for conversion into a giant park with tollbooths selling tickets for all the famous sights. Souvestre's tour of our planet in the year 3000 inaugurates futuristic dystopias with truly Orwellian vigor and consistency, but in a decidedly more comic mode than *Nineteen Eighty-Four*. Droll illustrations by Bertall, Penguilly, and St.-Germain enhance the comedy while also, and far from incidentally, providing the first extensive attempt to show how the future might look. Souvestre condemns technology as the means by which capitalism may imprison or destroy all humanity. *Le Monde tel qu'il sera* is science fiction's first great warning against the dangers of mechanization.

But that warning is blunted by Souvestre's heavy reliance on a satiric method of reductio ad absurdum that stresses the ridiculous more than the horrifying potential consequences of nineteenth-century mechanical "progress." In *Le Monde tel qu'il sera* satire veers so much in the direction of sheer comic exuberance of imagination that readers may amid their laughter find themselves sharing what is obviously Souvestre's fascination with the very possibilities that he deplores. To condemn with such hearty laughter is partly to condone. Paradoxically, therefore, Souvestre's pioneering masterpiece of futuristic technophobia has significant affinities with Verne's more overt technophilia.

So does the first book-length alternate history, another notable French breakthrough in exploration of science fiction's temporal dimension: Louis Geoffroy's *Napoléon et la conquête du monde—1812 à 1832—histoire de la monarchie universelle* (Napoleon and the conquest of the world—1812 to 1832—history of the universal monarchy, 1836). Also known as *Napoléon apocryphe* (The apocryphal Napoleon), this is an account of Napoleon's victorious Russian campaign, invasion of England, and establishment of a French monarchy that first governs Europe and later takes over the world. Toward the consequences of all this, Geoffroy is ambivalent. His alternative history of Napoleon triumphant is partly a devastating critique of the real Napoleon's blunders in Russia and of the Napoleonic system as a terrifyingly efficient police state in which, to our eyes, Napoleon seems a foreshadowing of Orwell's Big Brother while standing, for nineteenth-century readers, as an unmistakable warning against the dangers of any future superpower created along lines suggested by the historical Napoleon's ambitions. Partly too, however, Geoffroy's book is a Bonapartist's nostalgic utopia portraying a technologically advanced Francophone world that might have been had Napoleon avoided defeat in Russia. Chapters on how science flourished under Napoleon's universal monarchy survey developments that readers in 1836 would have accepted as a reasonably accurate portrait of their inevitable technological if not political destiny. Geoffroy's impossible alternative history that cannot occur in reality (because it did not) thus also sketches a very possible and possibly dangerous future of technological advances presented under the nonthreatening aegis of a past that never was.

In Geoffroy's Napoleonic world dirigibles are steered by a vaguely specified combination of magnetic forces and electricity. The power of steam engines has been increased 100-fold. Rapid locomotives cross the European part of Napoleon's vast empire in less than two days. Steamships with numerous paddlewheels cross the Atlantic in less than a week. Steam-powered earth-movers level mountains and dig canals. The weather is controlled by explosive devices that avert storms by dissipating clouds. Electric telegraphs link cities and continents in a "magical network" that allows instantaneous communication of information (and orders from the Emperor). Vaccines prevent the majority of diseases. There is a cure for blindness. A technique has been developed to render sea water potable by electricity combined with unspecified "other physical forces." The accelerating tempo of invention has resulted in what amounts to greater speed of thought itself, so that shorthand becomes the common notation and typewriters ("pianos d'écriture") are the usual instruments for quickly recording the new ideas that abound. Napoleon has especially encouraged geography, his favorite science, by including cartographers in the French armies that spread over the globe. To the few remote places unoccupied by Napoleon's troops France sends explorers to complete his great task of mapping the earth. A French admiral plants the tricolor at the North Pole.

If young Jules Verne, who was eight years old at the time of its publication in 1836, read *Napoléon*, he might have taken much inspiration from its pages. As if echoing while also amplifying Geoffroy, Verne's fiction dwells obsessively on powerful new machines, increasingly rapid travel, instantaneous telegraphic communication, voyages of exploration, details of cartography, and the wonders of electricity as a quasi-magical force. *Napoléon* might also have inspired Verne to consider the possibilities of alternative history, which is his preferred form although in a less obtrusive mode that typically introduces only one technological alternative per book instead of showing, as Geoffroy so boldly did, an entire world transformed politically no less than technologically. While going beyond Geoffroy and indeed beyond all his contemporaries in glorifying machinery, Verne was more cautious too, in preferring plots that refrain from proposing new political systems to accommodate technological advance. Verne's reluctance to imagine radical social change as the inevitable corollary of his futuristic machinery is something of a puzzle. A need to conform usually prevailed over Verne's almost equally insistent inclination to oppose the established order. Whatever the ultimate psychological and cultural causes of his conservative bent, the immediate stimulus for Verne's literary formula was provided by the publisher, Pierre-Jules Hetzel.

Anxious to reach a profitable market of younger readers together with their families and almost equally eager to remedy deficiencies in the scientific component of French education, Hetzel looked for appropriate books to publish and also in 1862 started a bimonthly periodical, the *Magasin illustré d'éducation et de récréation*, that soon numbered Verne among its contributors. As its title so emphatically proclaims to forestall any charges of frivolity, its aim was to achieve the traditional ideal of providing a dose of instruction rendered palatable by entertainment. Hetzel's focus on science made his project especially attractive to Verne, and vice versa. In 1863 Hetzel launched Verne's novelistic career by publishing *Cinq semaines en ballon* (*Five Weeks in a Balloon*), the first of those 63 "voyages extraordinaires" to which Verne gave the collective subtitle "Voyages in Known and Unknown Worlds." One of Hetzel's early advertisements announced that Verne's goal in this series was no less than "to outline all the geographical, geological, physical, and astronomical knowledge amassed by modern science and to recount, in an entertaining and picturesque format that is his own, the history of the universe."[9] Small wonder that Verne felt obliged to be prolific. His next six novels quickly staked out a claim to the realm of adventure laced with science: *Voyage au centre de la terre* (*Voyage to the Center of the Earth*, 1864); *De la terre à la lune* (*From the Earth to the Moon*, 1865); *Voyages et aventures du capitaine Hatteras* (*The Adventures of Captain Hatteras*, 1866); *Les Enfants du capitaine Grant* (*Captain Grant's Children*, 1867); *Vingt mille lieues sous les mers* (*Twenty Thousand Leagues Under the Sea*, 1870); and *Autour de la lune* (*Around the Moon*, 1870). Author and publisher collaborated to their great mutual profit until Hetzel's death in 1886. He acted as a conservative muse-cum-superego, sometimes actually censoring manuscripts and always restraining Verne in ways that pushed toward concealment his most dangerously oppositional impulses while encouraging his didactic penchant for combining lessons in science and history with adventures safely purged of dangerous women, sex, and overt attack on bourgeois values.

But thanks to Verne's talent for mythmaking his best work transcends pedagogy and subverts its own conservatism. It offers a two-stage experience for readers. Instruction and adventure are put in the foreground but then yield to symbolism in the service of a new "mythology of the Machine" that stays to haunt our imagination when his science lessons are forgotten; even didactic passages ultimately contribute to the power of Verne's myths because he marshals explanations of science into what Arthur Evans sums up as a sublime but reassuring epic of modern humanity merging with its machinery to conquer the elements and solve nature's riddles (Evans 1988, 14–15, 33). This great epic of reason and technology triumphant is Verne's master myth. It tends always toward familiarization of the unknown—"domestication of the strange . . . an attempt to restore the extraordinary to ordinariness" as Andrew Martin accurately characterizes this impulse—rather than, as in most science fiction of comparable impact, tending toward cognitive estrangement of the known.[10] Within Verne's comforting rather than alienating master myth, however, there are elements that allow his narratives to question sharply the social status quo that they ultimately uphold. Although Verne includes among his conservative strategies a sprinkling of ethnic and social stereotypes (of blacks, Jews, servants) that will (or should) grate on twentieth-century sensibilities, it is true, as Andrew Martin also notes, that Verne's "novels characteristically put their initial premisses in question. In particular, the powerful thrust of empire in Verne always attracts the countervailing force of revolt" (Martin, 22). Often too, Verne's romanticism undermines his overt stance as spokesman for scientific positivism with its comforting epistemology of a knowable universe in which everything may be understood and consigned to its place in our taxonomies. The outstanding example of Verne's complex artistry is his most famous novel.

Jules Verne: Twenty Thousand Leagues Under the Sea

First published serially in *Le Magasin illustré d'éducation et de récréation* from 20 March 1869 to 20 June 1870, *Twenty Thousand Leagues Under the Sea* was available as a separate book in two volumes by June 1870, just before the Franco-Prussian War started in July. After hostilities ended in 1871 other editions were printed to satisfy demand for a work whose central image of freedom and power embodied in Captain Nemo and his nearly invulnerable submarine appealed strongly to French readers shaken almost as much by political chaos during the Commune's seizure of Paris as by defeat at the hands of Prussia. But in applauding Verne's new myth of a marvelous warship contemporary French readers were not indulging in any mere fantasy of victorious nationalism. Quite the opposite. If the golden "N" against a black background on Nemo's personal flag evokes memories of Napoleon, it is only to dispel them as irrelevant except by way of contrast. "Nemo," which is Latin for "no one," "no man," "nobody," is only a pseudonym by which the captain chooses to be known, echoing the choice by Homer's Ulysses of "Nobody" as a name to deceive the Cyclops. It is not the imperial ambitions of Napoleon but the mythical wanderings of Ulysses to which the name "Nemo" invites comparison. It is not the tricolor that Verne's wily sailor plants at the South Pole but his black banner with golden "N," which ironically claims the Antarctic not for France but for Nobody. That, Verne implies, is as it should be.

Thus, far from offering vicarious enjoyment of astonishing feats performed by a French superman in aid of French or any other imperialism, *Twenty Thousand Leagues Under the Sea* more subversively tempts readers to admire a man without a country who has renounced allegiance to any of the earth's nations or their laws. Nor does Nemo follow even the accepted conventions of human society, to which he has abandoned all obligations except those of his own choosing. By insisting that in breaking with society he has become something other than what is usually meant by "a civilized man" despite his remarkable knowledge of arts and sciences, Nemo—and through him Verne—challenges us to reconsider our definitions of civilization.[11] When the French professor held captive aboard the *Nautilus* casually refers to Pacific islanders as savages, Nemo contemptuously refuses to acknowledge the customary unthinking distinction between savage and civilized places: "Savages! Where are there not any? Besides, are they worse than others, these whom you call savages?" (*TTL*, 257).

To Captain Nemo all governments merely represent varying degrees of institutionalized injustice. Against their shipping he has declared his own personal war. To what he takes as their savagery he replies with savagery of his own for reasons that are partly a matter of principled response to their oppressive actions and partly a matter of enacting some private revenge, which is only hinted at in a scene where after taking grim satisfaction in sinking a warship with all hands Nemo is glimpsed in his cabin sobbing over a picture of his dead wife and children. In addition to his depredations at sea he recovers sunken treasure to supply funds for arming revolutionaries ashore. But the full extent of such political involvement remains tantalizingly unspecified, as does his background. The aura of mystery with which Verne surrounds Nemo enhances his appeal as a romantic outcast in the Byronic mold, although as such he is more in the destructive line of romantic versions of Milton's Satan than of Byron's own reformist political engagement. Neither nationalist nor revolutionary in the usual senses, nor quite an anarchist either since he acts to counter or at least revenge injustice rather than simply to demolish governments, Nemo is finally described in apolitical terms as "a perfect archangel of hatred" (*TTL*, 490). Later, in *The Mysterious Island* (1874–75), probably as a gesture toward resurgence of nationalism in France after its defeat by Prussia, Verne dispels the mystery by disclosing that Nemo is an Indian prince angered at the suffering inflicted on his country by British imperialism. His motives thus remain anti-imperialistic while becoming more conventionally nationalistic.[12] *The Mysterious Island*, however, is best regarded as an altogether separate work that, like most sequels, is of interest in its own right but taken as a continuation merely diminishes effects achieved in its predecessor.

In *Twenty Thousand Leagues Under the Sea*, Verne presents Nemo as a champion of all the world's victims. After leaving a fortune in pearls with an impoverished Indian diver whom he has at great peril rescued from a menacing shark in a dangerous undersea battle, for example, Nemo explains his generous intervention by remarking that the diver is from the land of the oppressed and that he too will be "of that country" until his last breath. It is not India but a universal community of the dispossessed to which Nemo here declares allegiance (*TTL*, 311). In Nemo's cabin hang portraits of his heroes, all in their way fighters for freedom but none quite so alienated: Tadeusz Kościuszko, the Polish patriot who helped George Washington during the American Revolution; Marcos Botzaris, who fought for Greek Independence; the Irish patriot Daniel O'Connell; the deposed Italian leader Daniel Manin; Abraham Lincoln, the martyred emancipator; and the abolitionist John Brown—pictured on the gallows. Nemo has vowed never again to live on land. His element is the ocean's depths, to which he addresses an eloquent panegyric as a realm beyond the reach of despots, the only place where he or anyone can be truly free.

The means of achieving that freedom is the *Nautilus*. Verne thus makes this marvelous machine not only an emblem of human domination of nature and the instrument by which science is advanced as submarine exploration yields knowledge of regions hitherto denied to observation. The *Nautilus* is also an emblem of personal and political freedom. This lavishly furnished vehicle is at once a cozy nest for returning to the womb of the sea and a utopian refuge from the world's evils. Simone Vierne is right to insist that Verne's futuristic submarine is a polysemous image serving far more importantly as a symbol than as forecast of technological developments to come (*VML*, 40).

But of course the *Nautilus* is also extrapolation. Electricity of an unspecified sort is its secret motive force, of which Nemo will only say vaguely, "My electricity is not everybody's" (*TTL*, 178). This very special electricity, a leap to scientific fantasy, is the uncanny source of steady interior light, perfectly accurate chronometers, and power for engines that drive the *Nautilus* underwater at what are repeatedly described as "dizzying," "vertiginous" speeds of up to 50 miles per hour. This was far faster than surface ships could go in 1870 or than most can now go and remains an impressive and rarely attained underwater speed at the close of the twentieth century.

For Verne, as for so many later writers inside and outside science fiction, sheer velocity became an emblem of modern life. Rapid movement is a prominent feature of *Twenty Thousand Leagues Under the Sea* and much of Verne's other science fiction, which thus hints at ever-increasing acceleration as an inevitability for advanced technological societies. Verne has Nemo speculate, however, that given the ages it took for humanity to realize the force of steam, it may be more than a century before the world sees another *Nautilus*. This cautious forecast was not far off the mark. Electricity indeed became the primary motive force for actual undersea travel and remained so until a decade after Hiroshima, but diesel/electric submarines could not attain anything remotely approaching the underwater speed of Nemo's boat. Comparable (but not equal) velocity sustained under water over long distances was first achieved by its namesake, the American nuclear submarine *Nautilus* in 1955—close to the term of Nemo's prediction though only 85 years instead of a full century after *Twenty Thousand Leagues Under the Sea*. Verne deserves some credit for prophecy but mainly if Nemo's unusual electricity is retrospectively granted symbolic status as a forecast of atomic power (which in Verne's text it certainly is not).

Throughout Verne's narrative, prediction remains subordinated to symbolism. Among prominent features of the *Nautilus*, for example, though hardly intended as a forecast of amenities that will one day be found on every submarine, are two large compartments housing a museum and Nemo's vast library of twelve thousand volumes, described as suitable for a palace. On his spacious bookshelves are "all the finest works that mankind has produced in history, poetry, the novel, and science, from Homer to Victor Hugo, from Xenophon to Michelet, from Rabelais to Madame Sand" (*TTL*, 165). There are journals and books on mechanics, ballistics, hydrography, meteorology, geography, geology, and natural history. Scientific authors represented on Nemo's shelves include, we are told with humbling particularity, Humboldt, Arago, Foucault, Henri Sainte-Claire Deville, Chasles, Milne-Edwards, Quatrefages, Tyndall, Faraday, Berthelot, the Abbe Secchi, Petermann, Maury, Agassiz, "and more" (*TTL*, 166). Only works on political economy are absent, a telling omission that reveals Nemo's scorn—and Verne's—for what humanity had written about politics. In an equally spacious adjoining compartment serving as a gallery for copies of classic statues along with specimens of undersea plants, shells, and magnificent pearls, the walls are hung with thirty paintings by masters ranging from Raphael, Leonardo da Vinci, Correggio, Titian, and Holbein to Delacroix, Ingres, and their successors. Scattered around the big organ that Nemo plays to express himself when he is in a musical mood—usually late at night when most of the crew are asleep—there are scores by Weber, Rossini, Mozart, Beethoven, Haydn, Meyerbeer, Herold, Wagner, Auber, Gounod, and many others. Nemo's library and museum are partly an emblem—as indeed is Verne's entire oeuvre—of the positivist drive to acquire and organize knowledge. They reflect too the positivist conviction that valid knowledge of our universe *can* be achieved by science (Evans 1988, 38–41). The

Nautilus is a seagoing encyclopedia. Nemo's fabulous collection of art, music, and books makes his submarine an epitome of Western civilization up to the moment in 1865 when he took to the ocean.

A peculiar feature of Nemo's collections that renders them something other than merely or even primarily encyclopedic, however, is their conspicuous disorder, which Verne's narrative stresses: "Strange to say, all these books, in whatever language they were written, were indiscriminately arranged" (*TTL*, 165). So too for the music, and for the museum chamber in which "all the treasures of nature and art" are displayed "with the artistic confusion which distinguishes a painter's studio" (*TTL*, 168). Chance or aesthetics, not rational method, governs the arrangement though not the acquisition of Nemo's treasures. They are in random, not alphabetical, topical, or chronological order. By this deconstruction of positivist laws of taxonomy Verne transforms the account of his submarine museum into something very different from a mere pedagogic rehearsal of masters and masterpieces, a dreary lesson in cultural literacy. It becomes an invitation to move from history to myth.

Apologizing in his art gallery for "the disorder of this room," Nemo explains that since renouncing affiliation with the world ashore, which is now dead to him, everything from that world has in his view receded first into a distant past, and then into a timeless realm altogether outside history: "In my eyes, your modern artists are already old; they have two or three thousand years of existence; I confound them in my own mind. Masters have no age" (*TTL*, 171). All the musicians represented in his gallery, Nemo remarks, "are the contemporaries of Orpheus, for in the memory of the dead all chronological differences are erased. And I am dead" (*TTL*, 172). Even though its chronometers show Greenwich time for purposes of navigation, it is mythic time that reigns aboard the *Nautilus*. Mozart, Meyerbeer, and the rest coexist with Orpheus in Verne's land of the dead, as do Nemo and his crew along with their captives the French scientist Pierre Aronnax, his servant Conseil, and the Canadian harpooner Ned Land. So for a while do those readers who travel with them in imagination on what Aronnax calls "this extraordinary, supernatural, and incredible expedition" to Nemo's kingdom beneath the waves and beyond ordinary life (*TTL*, 108). His books, paintings, and other cultural artifacts have become symbols of initiation into a world beyond the ken of positivist orderings. Even the submarine's electricity, used not only for motive power but also to repel natives who try to attack the *Nautilus*, is referred to as transforming her into a kind of holy ark ("arche sainte"), which no one can profane without being struck down by thunder (*VML*, 245). To enter the *Nautilus* is thus to step outside time into myth, to journey like Orpheus from the upper world of the living to an underworld of the dead.

It is a paradox of this underworld created by technology that through its portholes one can observe but not quite participate in that teeming life of the ocean which Verne celebrates in visionary lyric passages describing strange sea creatures beautifully illuminated by the *Nautilus*'s marvelous electric lights. By such descriptions and related verbal painting of natural wonders in *Twenty Thousand Leagues Under the Sea*, and throughout his other novels, Verne uses science not as an end in itself but "as the logistical springboard to a Romantic contemplation of Nature . . . that is both enlightening and intrinsically poetic" (Evans 1988, 63). For Verne the machinery of science is thus ultimately justified on aesthetic rather than positivist grounds: for what it allows us to experience rather than for what it allows us to know or control. Most paradoxically of all, to board the *Nautilus* is to cross a threshold into a realm made sacred by secular technology. Of this shrine sanctified by science, the high priest is Nemo. Although fluent in seven European languages, with his crew he speaks an unknown tongue that becomes in effect a liturgical language.

Nemo's accidental acolyte is Verne's narrator, Pierre Aronnax. He too is a scientist whose specialty is the ocean, author of a treatise on marine biology entitled *Mysteries of the Great Depths of the Sea*. Here we have another pair reminiscent of Walton and Frankenstein. Instead of presenting readers with competing subjectivities as Mary Shelley does by having Victor Frankenstein *and* his monster each tell their tales within a narrative recorded by Walton and also giving his reactions, Verne retains the interplay of two differently gifted scientists but combines one of them with his monster/alter ego in the image of Nemo commanding the *Nautilus*, while providing only a single narration by the lesser scientist, Pierre Aronnax. Readers must decide whether to take

Nemo as simply a mad scientist, a more purposeful and accordingly even more dangerous intellectual descendant of Victor Frankenstein, with Aronnax playing the Waltonian role of sane although perhaps too approving observer who sympathetically though nevertheless damningly reports on the destructive activities of his more gifted but deranged counterpart. Or is Nemo's moral vision, that burning hatred of injustice that more than any Faustian desire for knowledge or power motivates his deployment of the *Nautilus*, to be taken as a sign of sanity in a politically deranged world? If so, we may excuse Nemo's excesses (and Aronnax's sympathy) as understandable reactions to the spectacle of unnecessary suffering inflicted on the weak by the strong and on the poor by the rich.

Nemo's moral sensitivity is as conspicuous as his ability to act ruthlessly when he deems it necessary. He even denounces wanton slaughter of whales as a typically human indulgence in killing for killing's sake that will eventually "annihilate a class of useful animals" (*TTL*, 401). In comparison Aronnax may seem not more sane but merely less imaginative. He is certainly less creative scientifically. He is utterly unable to invent or control a device like the *Nautilus*, although he is quick—perhaps too quick—to seize the opportunities it affords him for solving those mysteries of the sea that he also takes for his special area of investigation. Nemo's refusal to share his scientific discoveries by publishing them for humanity's benefit as Aronnax is eager to do raises yet other questions of intellectual responsibility where the comparison tilts more in favor of Aronnax. However we decide these issues, *Twenty Thousand Leagues Under the Sea* is a compelling variation on the urgent themes of *Frankenstein*.

It is also something of a psychological novel although not sufficiently credited as such because its narration by Aronnax instead of Nemo focuses so much on adventures, seascapes, and miscellaneous scientific explanations whose recounting illuminates the mentality of a narrator who is himself only a case of talent dangerously attracted into the orbit of genius. The inward turn of *Twenty Thousand Leagues Under the Sea* is further masked by the paradox that it reveals in most detail not Nemo's mind but that of a scientist who is accustomed to think mostly about the outward facts of what he observes and only fitfully resorts to more philosophical introspection during his captivity. Verne does not provide, as Shelley does in *Frankenstein*, the self-portrait of a superior mind endlessly interrogating itself and capable of inventing a whole new order of scientific menace. If Verne's shift of emphasis is not deliberately prophetic, it is at least symptomatic of an important transformation from the age of towering Newtonian individuality—run amok in the case of Victor Frankenstein—to the succeeding ages of science as a mass enterprise. While retaining Nemo as a romantic figure of isolated genius seen from a distance, Verne's confinement of narrative viewpoint to Aronnax makes his situation most accessible imaginatively. It is Aronnax's predicament, not Nemo's, with which we can most easily identify. Arguably, in the light of subsequent history, there is as much urgency in the less dramatic moral dilemmas confronted by those workaday scientists who, like Aronnax, must decide whether they are being lured across the boundary between research and transgression. The twentieth century's death camps and weapons laboratories have depended for their operation more on mediocrities like Walton and Aronnax than on those exercising the rare inventive capacities of Frankenstein and Nemo.

Because we always see Nemo from the outside we know something of what he says and does but must guess what he thinks. Nevertheless, insistent invitations to speculate about his thoughts add another important psychological dimension to what has too often been dismissed as a mere juvenile tale of adventure. There is, for example, that unforgettable moment, a small tour-de-force of romantic scene-setting, when Aronnax gives us a sketch of Nemo on the seafloor in his diving suit illuminated by the glare of an underwater volcano and "leaning on a mossy stone . . . motionless, as if petrified in mute ecstasy" while meditating amid the ruins of Atlantis: "Was he dreaming of the generations that had disappeared, and was he asking them the secret of human destiny? Was it here that this strange man came to steep himself in historical reminiscences, to relive this ancient life—he who wanted no modern one? What would I not have given to know his thoughts, to share them, to understand them! We remained for an entire hour at this place, contemplating the vast plain under the brightness of the lava" (*TTL*, 377). What readers are invited to contemplate in this scene is another departure from history to myth. Verne's ostensible science lesson has again drawn us across the boundary from the time and space described by positivism to that archetypal world of timeless human imagination where Orpheus coexists with lost Atlantis.

As Nemo and Aronnax leave "those ruins a thousand centuries old and contemporary with the geological epochs" the volcanic brightness gives way to another sublime effect: "the moon appeared through the mass of waters and threw pale rays on the buried continent" (*TTL*, 376–77). Whatever Nemo's inner life may be, it is only figured by outward signs that challenge interpretation, often ambiguously as here, where Atlantis becomes the opaque symbol of his attitude. Often too, we must even guess what he is doing because he conceals many of his activities from Aronnax, for whom Nemo is as much an ominous absence as a formidable presence.

It is part of the eerie Gothic atmosphere of life aboard the *Nautilus* that long intervals pass for its prisoners—who are entirely free to move about inside the ship—without a glimpse of Nemo or its crew, who always remain very ghostly figures mostly out of sight in their compartments or seen walking on the sea floor encased in diving suits that turn them into alien shapes with whom it is impossible to speak across the intervening water. Their private language renders them inaccessible aliens even when encountered face to face within the submarine. This impression of beings from elsewhere is articulated when Nemo finds another way of characterizing himself as alien in speaking not only of the *Nautilus* as a realm of the dead but as another planet: "a world apart . . . as foreign to land as the planets that accompany this globe around the sun" (*TTL*, 268). *Twenty Thousand Leagues Under the Sea* is the story of Aronnax's encounter with these alien places and creatures in unknown regions of his own world, an adventure that eventually becomes for him as much a psychological as a physical voyage of discovery.

Aronnax starts with a long account of widespread consternation caused in 1866 by sightings of what after much scientific debate is (incorrectly) taken for a whale or unknown variety of "sea monster." It soon begins to attack shipping. Some papers rush to print reminders of "every gigantic and imaginary creature, from the white whale, the terrible 'Moby Dick' of hyperborean regions, to the immense kraken, whose tentacles could entangle a ship of five hundred tons and drag it into the depths of the ocean" (*TTL*, 94). Other papers advise against "admitting the existence of krakens, sea serpents, 'Moby Dicks,' and other lucubrations of delirious sailors" (*TTL*, 95). These dismissive references relegating Herman Melville's imaginary white whale to the status of other fish stories serve two important purposes. Within the tale that Aronnax tells a sharp contrast is thus established between the absurdities of fiction and the realities of science, with the latter of course symbolized and given priority by the actuality of the *Nautilus*. Aronnax lives in a rational modern world where for serious people submarines replace krakens and anthropomorphized whales, and where fact must always displace myth. For readers of the novel that Jules Verne presents, these allusions to *Moby-Dick*, published in 1851, just nineteen years before *Twenty Thousand Leagues Under the Sea*, serve to challenge Aronnax's rational world by reestablishing the priority of myth over fact and imagination over positivism.

Placement of those allusions early in the first chapter of *Twenty Thousand Leagues Under the Sea* establishes one frame of reference for interpreting Verne's novel by inviting readers to compare and contrast it with Melville's great allegory. How closely, we must decide, *do* the parallels run between Aronnax and Ahab, Nemo's submarine and the white whale? The significance of Nemo, his *Nautilus*, and what they symbolize of the uses and abuses of technology, Verne implies, must ultimately be grasped in relation to ethical considerations best defined by such literature as *Moby-Dick* but excluded from science itself. And the choice is telling because Melville too presents a narrative where a vast amount of technical reportage—in his case teaching us in overwhelming factual detail, if we care to learn, the technology of the whaling industry—gives way to symbols that instruct us about perennial moral dilemmas. Were Verne's novel only or primarily a lesson in science (as Hetzel advertised it to be and as too many critics have incorrectly described it in order to dismiss it), it might better have been purged of any distracting allusions to other fiction. Instead it is filled with them. A complete list would suspiciously resemble the requirements for a Ph.D. qualifying exam in a first-rate department of comparative literature. Verne's method here and elsewhere is to embed his tales as much within the framework of other imaginative literature as within the accumulated fabric of scientific fact and theory. Andrew Martin notes that "few texts can have been quite so thoroughly permeated with other texts as Verne's" (Martin, 30). Certainly Verne was, as he claimed, more inclined than Wells to include scientific information. Its presence expands the length, slows the tempo, and provides a reading experience accordingly very different in texture from the powerful concision of Wells. But Verne at his best was no less able to provide effective works of the mythic imagination, not mere scientific reportage topped with a layer of story.

Verne's myths for the modern world, even more often than those of Wells, are explicitly affiliated to their literary antecedents. Thus early evocation of Homer's Ulysses by Nemo's name, and allusions to Melville's epic of the ocean at the outset of *Twenty Thousand Leagues Under the Sea* are matched at its end by allusion to Edgar Allan Poe. As Aronnax nears the final moments of his voyage he finds himself in a literally and even more eerily timeless realm: "The clocks had been stopped on board. It seemed, as in polar countries, that night and day no longer followed their regular course. I felt myself being drawn into that strange region where the overworked imagination of Edgar Poe roamed at will. Like the fabulous Gordon Pym, at every moment I expected to see 'that veiled human figure, of larger proportions than those of any inhabitant of earth, thrown across the cataract which defends the approach to the pole'" (*TTL*, 491). Here Aronnax rightly senses himself in a "strange region" of a very different order from the physical remoteness of the ocean's depths. He has crossed a psychological threshold to an area of the mind occupied with tasks very different from recording new facts of marine biology. Just as Verne's initial allusions to the white whale paid homage to *Moby-Dick* as one inspiration for *Twenty Thousand Leagues Under the Sea* while suggesting too a literary analogue, he here acknowledges Poe's influence while also suggesting another work that can serve readers as a point of comparison for deciphering the meaning of Aronnax's encounter with Nemo—though no easy key, because *The Narrative of A. Gordon Pym* (1837) ends inconclusively. Much impressed by Poe, and author of an essay in 1864 praising his attempts to mingle unusual settings with strange effects, Verne was so teased by *The Narrative of A. Gordon Pym* that he later wrote a novel continuing it: *Le sphinx des glaces* (*An Antarctic Mystery*, 1897).

These framing allusions at the outset and conclusion of *Twenty Thousand Leagues Under the Sea* are also invitations to stand back from the science lessons and appraise Verne's artistry. The effect is similar to that of the equally self-reflexive invitation from Wells's Time Traveller to evaluate his tale not for its truth but for its aesthetic appeal: "taking it as a story, what do you think of it?"[13] To answer that question with reference to *Twenty Thousand Leagues Under the Sea*, Verne audaciously suggests, the proper touchstones include the *Odyssey*, *Moby-Dick*, and *The Narrative of A. Gordon Pym* as well as a host of other works alluded to less conspicuously. The network of allusion finally shifts judgment of *Twenty Thousand Leagues Under the Sea* from assessment of its accuracy as scientific reportage and usefulness as a science lesson or as prophecy to assessment of its artistic merits by comparison with its literary predecessors and peers. As always in the best imaginative literature, but even more explicitly in Verne's narrative than in most, mimesis gives way to intertextuality. What at first seems to be a mirror held up to nature becomes at last a magical looking-glass through which we pass to the wonderland of art.

Although not literally accurate, the word "monster" is at the outset applied so frequently (34 times) to what turns out to be the *Nautilus* that on a metaphoric level Verne's identification of it as a monster is unmistakable (*VML*, 37). A telling difference is that it is a technological rather than biological monstrosity. Invited to join a hunt for this threatening creature aboard an American warship, the USS *Abraham Lincoln* (ironically named to honor one of Nemo's heroes), Aronnax inexplicably discovers his destiny: "Three seconds after reading the letter of the Honorable Secretary of the Navy I understood at last that my true vocation, the sole end of my life, was to hunt this disturbing monster and purge it from the world" (*TTL*, 104). Here Aronnax responds like another Ahab. But the resemblance dissolves into ironic contrasts. He does not purge the monster: it swallows him and he finds himself to a disturbing degree sharing its outlook. Its end, if indeed it comes to an end, is not brought about by Aronnax. Lest we miss the irony of inevitable comparisons with Jonah, Verne has Aronnax exclaim just before being taken aboard the *Nautilus*,

"The time is past for Jonahs to take refuge in whales' bellies!" (*TTL*, 135). But the time has *not* passed. It is only the nature of whales and Jonahs that has changed, thanks to "progress." The metaphoric equivalences of submarine and whale, Aronnax and Jonah, which point to important dimensions of ethical significance, further blur what *Twenty Thousand Leagues Under the Sea* apparently, but only at first glance, presents as displacement of legendary ambiguities by the certainties of positivist science.

After a series of mishaps Aronnax is taken prisoner by the *Nautilus* off Japan on 7 November 1867, along with Conseil and Ned Land. Nemo (the great champion of freedom) vows never to release them, hoping thus to prevent disclosure of his secrets. He offers the dubious consolation, most appealing to Aronnax's scientific curiosity but regarded with horror by Ned Land and indifference by Conseil, of endless investigation of the sea. What follows are Aronnax's recollections of his unexpected voyage with Nemo across the Pacific to the Indian Ocean, thence via a secret underground waterway paralleling the Suez Canal to the Mediterranean, out into the Atlantic, through icefields to the South Pole, and eventually to Norwegian waters, where toward the end of June 1868, Aronnax escapes with Conseil and Ned Land at their urging just before the *Nautilus* is dragged down to an unknown fate by the notorious Maelstrom—featured too in Poe's 1841 short story "A Descent into the Maelström"—while the three escapees take refuge with hospitable fishermen on the Lofoten Islands. Amid these northern waters above the Arctic Circle, in a setting reminiscent both of Poe and of Walton writing from polar regions at the edge of space about another scientist and monster, and with something like the evocative power of Shelley's setting, Aronnax completes his narrative.

His account directs attention both outward and inward. It invites us to look at marvelous glimpses of beautiful underwater life and scenery viewed from within the speeding *Nautilus* and viewed too while on underwater excursions from it in diving suits with portable air tanks. It rivets attention on such action as Nemo's combats with warships, with sharks, and (most famously) with a giant squid. It invites us to attend the bizarre but moving underwater funeral of a crew member killed in one of Nemo's mysterious battles. It invites us to contemplate not only the ruins of Atlantis but again and again the less mythic debris of sunken ships (including remains of the lost La Pérouse expedition) and other technojunk that litters the seabed as an ironic measure of human progress. There are dozens of passages, many quite long and detailed, supplying scientific or historical information. In them Verne strives to meet the educational goal set by Hetzel while nevertheless subordinating their facts to narrative purposes. They are also attempts to familiarize strange areas of our world rather than to defamiliarize the known. Less often remarked but also important in the economy of Verne's narrative is its inner drama of Aronnax's progressive identification with Nemo, which makes him reluctant to join his comrades in attempting escape.

Aronnax confesses at one point after throwing cold water on an escape plan that "admiring the *Nautilus,* I was incarnated in the skin of her captain" (*VML,* 304: "fanatique du *Nautilus,* j'étais incarné dans la peau de son commandant"). Pushing aside any sense of obligation to help free the other prisoners, Aronnax is increasingly reluctant to abandon his only chance to conduct firsthand research that may allow him (somehow, someday) to publish a more complete and accurate edition of his book on the mysteries of the depths. In itself this desire to stay and learn is harmless. But it isolates Aronnax from his companions, who are after all his community. Conseil, although finally more than willing to leave, professes himself content to stay wherever his master is, amusing himself (and readers) by classifying fish with tediously pedantic accuracy. The absurdity of his pointless taxonomic hobby is another of Verne's satiric subversions of that scientific positivism which in its more soberly didactic moments his story seems intended to affirm. The harpooner Ned Land, whose profession is to kill, not study, the ocean's life, counts his undersea voyage as a total waste of time and thinks only of ways to get ashore. After Aronnax is at last persuaded to escape by the others, which he does as reluctantly as he first came aboard the *Nautilus,* his final comments on the meaning of his experience— the last words of *Twenty Thousand Leagues Under the Sea*—are an ambiguous affirmation of identification with Nemo as though only they two had actually experienced the voyage: "And to the question asked by Ecclesiastes 6000 years ago: 'Who has ever been able to fathom the depths of the abyss?' two men alone of all now living have the right to give an answer: Captain Nemo and myself" (*TTL*, 499). In becoming another Nemo, if only a less domineering and less inventive version, as well as by traveling with him, Aronnax has plumbed not merely the ocean's depths but a moral abyss from which only he returns, and that unwillingly. For readers Verne poses the challenge of fathoming both depths.

Aliens, Androids, and Icons

If Verne's protagonists moving restlessly around, above, and within the earth are not much shaken by Pascalian dread of those infinite spaces beyond our planet, neither are they inclined to define their existence by Cartesian introspection. Even the often meditative Nemo, into whose mind Aronnax finds himself drawn as into another abyss, a mental maelstrom, is finally defined not by what he thinks but by what he does as commander of the *Nautilus*, and by what it does and where it goes. Instead of a Cartesian cogito (I think, therefore I am), the Vernian model of science fiction is grounded in empiricist affirmation that to exist is to roam over our world and other worlds to observe: I explore, therefore I am. But Descartes is also the founder of analytical geometry. Of this mathematical side of Cartesian rationalism that is supremely concerned with spatial representation of relationships, and as much a hallmark of French culture as Cartesian introspection, Verne's writing may indeed be the archetypal imaginative expression: the fiction par excellence of geometry, always inviting us to trace imaginary lines around our globe and into (and back from) the space through which it and its satellite trace their complex orbits. The action of Verne's plots can almost always be diagrammed as lines on a geometric grid, and the patterns thus traced reveal much about the significance of his narratives.

As for Pascalian terror, Barbicane in *Around the Moon* experiences a few bad moments en route to and from the moon, most notably when he considers the possibility, "filled with all the terrors of the infinite," that he and his companions in their projectile will neither land on the moon nor return to earth, but instead disappear forever into the uncharted regions of interstellar space along some arc that has no end and cannot be diagrammed with reference to known coordinates.[14] Nevertheless Barbicane and his fellow astronauts, especially the "audacious" Frenchman Michel Ardan—modeled on the pioneering photographer and balloonist Félix Tournachon (known as Nadar), but who also stands for Verne himself—more frequently occupy themselves with practical tasks of scientific observation to improve lunar cartography. They also gaze with pleasure, not fright—pleasure that the narration invites us to share—out the porthole of their cozy spaceship to admire the stars that serve as a magnificent backdrop for the moon: "The imagination loses itself in that sublime infinity, in the midst of which the projectile moved like a new star created by the hand of humanity. . . . these stars were gentle eyes gazing in that profound night amid the absolute silence of space" (*ADLL*, 159; my translation). Here the silence of those infinite spaces is soothing. The nineteenth-century optimism of *Around the Moon* marks a recovery, however temporary, from Pascalian terror.

But Verne draws back from space just as he avoids the future. His protagonists never take a leap very far from earth into that infinity beyond our solar system. They do not even land on the moon. The protagonists of *Hector Servadac* (1877) find themselves in space but only on a big chunk of the earth that has been drawn away by a passing comet. It remained for others to populate Verne's beautiful, placid, silent universe with aliens, and to question the nature of that human intelligence which contemplates the sublime spectacle.

In *Les Xipéhuz* (*The Xipehuz*, 1887), J.-H. Rosny Aîné (the Elder) (pseudonym of Joseph-Henri Honoré Boëx, 1856–1940) introduced truly alien aliens: creatures of crystalline composition animated by electromagnetic energy, communicating via strange symbols projected onto each other by light beams, and able to change shapes from cylindrical to leaflike to conical.[15] To humans these aliens remain incomprehensible. No dialogue is ever established. In positing an utterly different physical basis for what is undeniably a form of intelligent life, although chemically unlike our own and with a correspondingly enigmatic psychology, Rosny made a notable step toward speculative xenobiology. He broke away from the hallowed Lucianic tradition of allegorical aliens whose traits are defined largely for satiric or utopian purposes of social commentary rather than on a basis of scientific speculation. Nevertheless *The Xipehuz* is not set somewhere out in the galaxy, but here on earth in prehistoric times to dramatize a Darwinian competition for survival of the fittest between humans and their rival life form, the Xipehuz. In what also has the less praiseworthy distinction of being a classic of dreary xenophobia, Rosny's narrative recounts for our applause the clever stratagems by which its protagonist first studies the enemy with the cool detachment of a protoscientist to find their weak spots, then with the military genius of a proto-Napoleon leads the combined tribes of humanity to annihilate the Xipehuz and inherit the planet. This outcome is presented as an altogether happy ending: good riddance to the Xipehuz. Rosny's tale does not encourage any more complex moral than the importance of being clever enough to kill off threatening aliens that we do not understand. It is of course an equally happy day for readers when H. G. Wells's invading Martians are destroyed by earth's bacteria (no thanks to its generals). But *The War of the Worlds* is far more concerned to invite speculation about the philosophical implications of hostile—or other—aliens that cannot be reduced to mirror images of ourselves and who give us a taste of our own poisonous political medicine. In fairness to Rosny, however, whose career extended well into the twentieth century, I should note too that he turned the tables in 1910 with *La Mort de la terre* (The death of the earth), in which mineral-based creatures (the ferromagnétaux) triumph over humans. In *Les Navigateurs de l'infini* (Navigators of the infinite, 1925), Rosny makes Mars the site of human interactions with aliens, including a pioneering human-alien love affair, possibly the first in science fiction.[16]

Of all nineteenth-century science fiction, *L'Eve future* (*Tomorrow's Eve*, 1886) by Auguste de Villiers de l'Isle-Adam (1838–89) most acutely takes up the Cartesian cogito to explore its implications for defining the borderline separating humanity from other forms of existence. Villiers boldly appropriates for fiction a real and still living scientist by taking as his protagonist, Thomas Alva Edison (1847–1931). Villiers justifies this move in a preface explaining that Edison's inventions such as the phonograph and incandescent light bulb (Villiers also gives him credit for the telephone) have already turned him into a legend in the popular mind—called among other laudatory terms "The

Magician of the Century," "The Sorcerer of Menlo Park"—and hence a figure who, *as a legend*, already belongs no less than Faust "to the world of literature." Villiers specifies that in *Tomorrow's Eve* he aims to "interpret a modern legend to the best advantage of the work of Art-metaphysics that I have conceived, and that, in a word, the hero of this book is above all 'The Sorcerer of Menlo Park,' and so forth—and not the engineer, Mr. Edison, our contemporary."[17] By noting that his story is not about science but about a legend of science, Villiers articulates here for the first time a distinction crucial to science fiction but still seldom appreciated by its critics and readers although intuited by most of its authors. He is not concerned with the real Edison, or his real science, as material for fiction, but rather with taking a new mythology of science—the rapidly evolved myth of Edison the engineer as wonder worker—and exploring both the aesthetic and philosophical uses of that myth. Villiers understood that literature may be about science but is more properly about our perceptions of science. The latter, most often, is the true subject of science fiction, especially the best science fiction, which is less frequently concerned with actual science than with creating or appropriating legends of science to explore its role in our lives and its empowerment of our art.[18]

The imaginary Edison presented by Villiers has worked in his secret underground laboratory to create a mechanical woman, an android named Hadaly, animated by electrical motors and speaking via a phonograph stocked with various phrases that may be appropriately programmed to particular circumstances. This project is aimed at duplicating the human body while improving on it via mechanical, not biological, means. Edison has also been working in the tradition of Mesmer to study the mind via hypnotic experiments with a woman, Mrs. Anny Anderson, who has experienced a terrible series of psychic traumas at the hands of a brutal and unfaithful husband, and who has fallen into a cataleptic trance. By means of hypnotism Edison reaches a being called Sowana while talking with, or trying to talk with, Mrs. Anderson. It is a strength of *Tomorrow's Eve* that Sowana's ultimate nature and significance remain ambiguous: she may be some facet of Mrs. Anderson's mind, a part of what we would call her unconscious; or she may be another entity altogether, somehow attainable through the medium of Mrs.

Anderson's mentality. At one level Sowana represents feminine and artistic ideals difficult if not impossible to achieve in actuality. Whatever her nature and import, however, Sowana no less than the mechanical android is explained as a natural phenomenon although far more elusive to scientific investigation than those motor and vocal mechanisms of the human body that may be duplicated in a machine like Hadaly. *Tomorrow's Eve* anticipates Freudian concern with relationships between conscious and unconscious areas of the mind while also posing fundamental questions about the interaction of mind and matter.

While in the midst of these experiments with mind and body, Edison is visited by an English friend, Lord Celian Ewald, who is about to commit suicide in despair at the banal stupidity of his mistress, the ravishingly beautiful actress Alicia Clary. He is disillusioned to the point of existential nausea at human life by finding that the world's most beautiful woman, who looks exactly like the Louvre's Venus de Milo, is the world's most boring creature: empty, shallow, and utterly unable to provide intellectual companionship. Aphrodite in the flesh, this one at least, is intolerable. Edison first comforts Ewald after a fashion by confirming his misogyny with a rather Swiftian tale of an even more shocking situation of female duplicity involving a gorgeous but depraved as well as stupid woman who lured a man (Mrs. Anderson's husband) to infidelity, disease, and destruction, although (unlike Alicia Clary) her beauty was achieved entirely by makeup and clothing. As an alternative to suicide for Lord Ewald, Edison proposes finishing Hadaly to duplicate the appearance, mannerisms, and voice of Alicia so that Ewald can discard her in favor of living with a creature equally charming but *known* to be a mere machine and therefore not likely to disappoint because arousing no expectations of anything higher than mechanical responses. The pleasures of the flesh will be discarded as will, apparently, all pretense of a mind within the body. Edison's deplorably misogynist premise is that his android will be more satisfactory than any real woman could possibly be: technophilia in excelsius.

Ewald is intrigued but of course doubts that Edison can succeed in exactly duplicating Alicia. He doubts too that such a genuinely mindless duplicate, if it were made, could ever be a satisfactory companion. Edison challenges him to try the result, insisting (like a protobehaviorist) that with sufficiently complex and random programming Hadaly will be indistinguishable *from the outside*, i.e., by Ewald, from a real woman. To the observer, in other words, her—or anyone's—behavior, if sufficiently human-like, will achieve the status of an actual person. Art—in the form of Edison's science—will improve on life. It will not matter to Hadaly's companions that she has no sentience if she acts in every way as though she did. In this challenge and in its dramatic denouement, Villiers goes far beyond the novel's layer of Swiftian distaste for women, and beyond, too, romantic symbolism using Hadaly and Alicia as counters to show the interplay of reality and unattainable ideals.

By the confrontation of Lord Ewald with the completed Hadaly, who is at their first interview so perfect in her imitation of a human (including artificial flesh indistinguishable from real flesh) that Ewald mistakes her for Alicia, Villiers probes the issue of how far both actual self-awareness—the Cartesian cogito—and the perception by others of what they take for behavioral evidence of that cogito are necessary to existence as a living creature. In *L'Homme machine* (Man the machine, 1747) Julien Offroy de La Mettrie had proposed that people are machines. Villiers proposes that machines can be people. What complicates his fable beyond this simple but effective inversion of an Enlightenment paradox is that Hadaly somehow *acquires* sentience to become something (but what?) very different from a mere robot carrying out a program, however intricate and partially random in its pattern to duplicate the apparent randomness of human behavior. Ewald is pleasantly shocked to discover that the beautiful machine has indeed transcended the human beauty on which it was modeled by its scientist-creator. Edison concludes that Hadaly has become a receptacle for the entity known to him as Sowana. As Hadaly acquires sentience, Mrs. Anderson slips from her cataleptic trance into death. But what has actually happened? Has some unconscious part of her mind made a transition to full awareness in Edison's android, endowing the machine with human existence? Or, as the text also hints, has some other form of mentality that needs a human or human-like mechanism for incorporation manifested itself first via Mrs. Anderson's neural network and then via the electrical network that powers Hadaly? Has this alien mentality, whether from Mrs.

Anderson's unconscious—that is, from the hidden part of a real woman's mind—or from elsewhere, some ideal realm of the spirit, been summoned into existence by a man's longing for ideal womanhood? All the complexities of Villiers's subtle novel cannot be dealt with here, and they are barely suggested by what I have said about its plot. For the history of science fiction what stands out in this still very challenging tale is its artistically coherent introduction without recourse to the supernatural of speculation about possible relationships between thought, mechanism, and life.

Villiers takes newly minted legends of Edison the wonder-working mesmerist and mechanician as a basis not for instruction about real possibilities of science, but in the Wellsian manner of "scientific patter" for giving verisimilitude to an invention—the android—far beyond Edison's actual capacity and also far beyond anything likely to be achieved during his lifetime or for several lifetimes to come, if ever. Villiers, however, maximizes scientific patter. More than for Wells's brief explanations of the time machine, or Frankenstein's vaguely described biological experiments, and more than for the special but never explained electricity that drives Nemo's submarine, Villiers plies readers with quasi-scientific explanations of how Hadaly is built up bit by bit: how a phonograph inside her chest works to produce her speech; how internal motors control her movements; how her lifelike "flesh" is made; and how via elaborate photography and phonograph recordings very precise measurements of Alicia Clary's appearance, mannerisms, and speech patterns are taken to serve as templates for these aspects of the android. As with Nemo's submarine, but with far more pseudoscientific detail, the results are made to seem for readers something that science *could* conceivably bring into being, and with this granted, philosophical and other issues arising from that possibility are explored. Verne creates verisimilitude primarily by surrounding with lessons in real science his one key speculative leap to a new kind of electricity and thence to the imaginative core of *Twenty Thousand Leagues Under the Sea*: the *Nautilus* with all its powers. Villiers starts with a series of speculative leaps that are referred to real science only indirectly via allusion to popular images of Edison, whose legendary achievements thus provide verisimilitude for the world created in *Tomorrow's Eve*. This is a world like our own governed by natural laws, not magic, and in every way resembling that of 1886 except that androids like Hadaly are possible. It is a world where machines may achieve sentience. They think, and therefore they are our companions.

Going beyond both Verne and Villiers, Albert Robida (1848–1926) brought French science fiction into the mode that has prevailed in the twentieth century by dropping all concern with technical explanations or even the appearance of technical explanations, focusing instead on the accomplishments of marvelous scientific machines themselves—*what* they can do, not how they do it—in order to depict not isolated incidents such as the intrusion into our present of futuristic technology like Hadaly, the *Nautilus*, or Robur's airships, but the accumulation of such machines to produce a future world whose sociology is determined by its technology.[19] Whereas Verne shrank from the future, Robida embraced it.[20] He was also a superb artist whose illustrations gave that future an immediacy that no previous future had attained. To be sure, Robida built on foundations laid by the fantastic artist Grandville (Jean-Ignace-Isidore Gérard, 1803–47); by Félix Bodin's call for a *littérature futuriste*; by Souvestre's profusely illustrated dystopia *Le Monde tel qu'il sera*; by France's preeminent role in the emergence of futuristic fiction during the eighteenth and early nineteenth century; and above all by the hundreds of illustrations that were for nineteenth-century readers an integral part of their experience with Verne's texts. Illustrated editions of his extraordinary voyages, along with the nineteenth-century vogue of book illustrations more generally, had taught readers to visualize the worlds of their fiction. But these were past and present worlds with at most a few new features hinting at the shape of things to come. Robida taught readers to look as well as think ahead. He was the first to achieve an imaginatively coherent and very complete iconography of the future.

With Robida the characteristic self-referentiality of science fiction also becomes very conspicuous. To science, the impact of science, and legends of science as science fiction's master topics once the genre emerges as a distinct form must be added science fiction itself. Robida made this addition. Verne's blend of science with adventure, although not entirely unique, had achieved sufficient popularity to establish distinctive conventions that could themselves become a subject of fiction. Ending as a satirist, Robida began as a parodist by publishing serially *Les Aventures très extraordinaires de Saturnin Farandoul dans les 5 ou 6 parties du monde et dans tous les pays connus et même inconnus de Monsieur Jules Verne* (The very extraordinary adventures of Saturnin Farandoul in the 5 or 6 parts of the world and in all the countries known and unknown of Mr. Jules Verne, 1879–82). From this Robida proceeded to *Le Vingtième siècle* (The twentieth century, 1883); *La Guerre au XXe siècle* (War in the twentieth century, 1883, and 1887 in another version); *Jadis chez aujourd'hui* (The past at home in the present, 1890), a tale of luminaries from the past brought to see the present, which dismays them; *Voyage de fiançailles au XXe siècle* (The fiancé's trip in the twentieth century, 1892), describing a premarital honeymoon set in 1954; *La Vie électrique* (The electrical life, 1893), a continuation of *Le Vingtième siècle*; *L'Horloge des siècles* (The clock of the centuries, 1902), a tale of time reversal; and *L'Ingénieur von Satanas* (Engineer Von Satanas, 1919), a sober response to World War I. There are no English translations of these nor is it easy to find copies of Robida's books, but a 1981 Slatkine reprint of *Le Vingtième siècle* has again brought this masterpiece within reach.[21]

Its illustrations of life in the 1950s now have at first glance a misleading air of antiquated anticipation that makes them seem rather off the mark as prediction (see the following illustrations for examples). But Robida's pictures of aircraft, television (téléphonoscope) sets, and other twentieth-century technology seem quaint because they were designed to seem faintly or (most often) more than faintly preposterous in order to satirize the very tendencies of mechanical progress that they exemplify. Another source of misleading quaintness to our eyes is Robida's frequent juxtaposition of futuristic gadgets with people in very conspicuously nineteenth-century costumes in order to satirize a disturbing lag between mechanical and social progress. To appreciate the remarkable narrative as well as the predictive and satiric force of Robida's illustrations they must be regarded in conjunction with his text, into which they are closely integrated. Almost everything mentioned in the story is illustrated for readers to see, thus building up for the first time in science fiction an equivalent to the now familiar cinematic experience of visual participation in narrated events. Robida thus establishes an

Le Théatre chez soi par le téléphonoscope (Theater at his home via television)

Le journal téléphonoscopique (Television news)

Sur les toits (On the roofs)

Station centrale des aéronefs a Notre-Dame (Central airship station at Notre-Dame Cathedral)

Aéronefs-omnibus de la compagnie genérale (Air-bus of the General Company)

Révolution de 1953: Le Bataillon de la suprématie féminine arrivant aux barricades (Revolution of 1953: battalion of feminine supremacy arrives at the barricades)

La lune rapprochée: départ de la première commission scientifique et colonisatrice (The moon drawn closer to earth: departure of the first scientific and colonizing expedition)

iconography of the future that, like later versions presented in films and comic strips, can also be recalled as an imaginative aid by readers as they encounter and mentally visualize different texts. Once the basic icons of aircraft and television—or in later works spaceships, phasers, blasters, and whatnot—have been established as indicators of a future setting, even partial descriptions of these items will recall them sufficiently for many purposes of temporal location ahead in time while serving also to link texts with bonds of familiar conventions.

Although it is true that Robida lacks Verne's ability to create suspense in plots whose characters and machines become powerful myths, Robida nevertheless deserves far more recognition than he has received as a skillful narrator and a prose stylist of considerable versatility. His forte is comedy with a satiric punch. The story told in *Le Vingtième siècle* is at once a self-reflexive parody of its own Vernian preoccupation with marvelous machinery, a parody in the manner of Souvestre of futuristic utopias in general, a sharp satire aimed at nineteenth-century optimism about the advantages of scientific progress, and rather surprisingly for such a parodic style, ultimately a shrewd prediction about many actual tendencies of highly industrialized societies. The world thus presented by Robida in deliberately absurdist images is uncomfortably like our own all too absurd reality.

By the 1950s of Robida's *Le Vingtième siècle* a devastating world war has come and gone with remarkably little effect on the triviality of subsequent social attitudes within Western countries preoccupied with making money and having a good time. France, headed by a robot-president ("Président Mécanique") is about to become a joint-stock corporation with stockholders instead of citizens. Meanwhile political parties stage mock revolutions every ten years complete with storming of ingenious Parisian barricades (purchased at an international barricade exposition hawking the latest wares). Only blank bullets are fired. Thus everyone (including tourists) can safely enjoy a picturesque spectacle with nostalgic echoes of France's great revolutionary moments in the eighteenth and nineteenth centuries, while actually participating in politics reduced to an entertaining sham. Journalists covering real wars with immense casualties in Asia become celebrities with devoted fans. Criminals are absolved of responsibility for crimes mostly regarded as the result of unfortunate family circumstances, and they are rehabilitated in luxurious prisons. New historicists ("La nouvelle école historique") are busy revising history. Racine and other classics of the French theater are presented in grotesquely modernized versions. Italy has been purchased by entrepreneurs for transformation into a European park (a giant proto-Disneyland) featuring a reconstruction of Pompeii populated by actors in period costumes. Contemporary architecture is a fantasia of styles imitating those of various historical periods according to the whims of builders: the past has become nothing more significant than a supermarket of decors.

Music, drama, entertaining shows, and an endless stream of horrifying news items are always available on television. Correspondence and face-to-face meetings are rare because all business (including proposal, marriage, and divorce) can more easily be conducted via telephone by people who are always in a hurry. Advertisements are everywhere, including ads from the many matrimonial agencies active in matching up eligible singles, who can no longer easily meet each other on their own. Fast-food kitchens pipe their produce to every well-heeled home, sometimes with disastrous results when a soup pipe bursts flooding a dining room, and sometimes with other problems as when a cook falls into a giant stew pot to become part of the evening's puree. But such industrial accidents never impede business. Rapid transit by air and underground rail allow everyone to keep in perpetual motion. Robida makes images of aerial travel within and between cities and countries the great emblem of his future just as in the first half of the twentieth century spaceships became a universal icon of the future.

Readers tour Robida's future to discover its alarming aspects along with his attractive but naïve and impoverished orphan protagonist Hélène Colobry (herself a figure parodying romantic novels) after she arrives in Paris from a secluded country high school. Her guardian and uncle, the wealthy banker Raphaël Ponto, introduces her to society and various career prospects. Hélène, altogether lazy, uninterested in domestic politics including the powerful feminist movement, and incurious about foreign wars that are a disturbing staple of the inescapable téléphonoscope, is horrified to find that in an age of liberated women she is apparently doomed to earn a living by hard work. Ponto gets her started, to no avail, as a barrister, as a journalist, as a politician, and as a writer. After what we but not she find amusing struggles in these various spheres of modern life she is dispatched to retrieve Ponto's son Philippe from imprisonment in England, where Mormon authorities, overlooking his French citizenship, have zealously relegated him to a dungeon reserved for stubborn bachelors who refuse to marry their share of wives. England has succumbed to the strong lure of fundamentalist primitivism in the twentieth century by discarding as its state religion the Anglican Church in favor of old-style patriarchal Mormonism. After this episode of a theocratic sexual dystopia within the larger dystopia of twentieth-century life, Robida parodies the happy endings of romantic fiction by allowing the wealthy Philippe to fall in love with Hélène. Their marriage does not wind up the plot as in conventional romances, however. The plot closes by parodying the Vernian journey with a honeymoon tour of the world via airship and submarine yacht.

After the submarine is sunk by a mine left over from the world war, one of many drifting around in shipping lanes, Hélène and Philippe embark too on a Vernian Robinsonade by taking refuge with the submarine's captain and crew on an artificial island, one of a chain of such devices anchored to accommodate distressed sailors. But the island is cut loose by savages, who then flee leaving the honeymoon party to jury-rig sails and a rudder and sail the artificial island toward Tahiti, where they are again shipwrecked but finally rescued. All this inspires Philippe with the idea of forming a European company to construct a sixth continent in Polynesian waters. Le Vingtième siècle ends not on the traditional comic note of marriage but with a switch of tone from satire to serious description of the titanic enterprise of constructing and populating the new continent. A way is also found of drawing the moon closer to the earth in order to provide better nighttime illumination. Terraforming—but of our own planet— is the grandiose vision that Robida somewhat illogically grafts onto his satire, thus turning its apparent technophobia into explicit technophilia.

But the shift is less incoherent than it may seem when abstractly described because, as in Souvestre's Le Monde tel qu'il sera, Robida's satire against the world created by technology is so lighthearted in tone as to elicit more affectionate than derisive laughter. His amusement is tempered by love for his absurd machines, a love that it is hard for any but the most humorless reader not to share. Robida's accuracy in predicting the twentieth century via his farcical plot has been something of an embarrassment to critics who (like myself) insist that the best science fiction uses its futures mainly as tropes for discussing the present. Thus Marc Angenot ruefully observes that there is "a problem with Robida's fantasies, something that is always acknowledged with amused amazement but never accounted for: Robida is the only nineteenth-century SF writer to invent a picture of our century which is never fundamentally wrong; his ironically pessimistic predictions have by and large proved to be *true*, in an unequalled degree of soundness and complexity."[22] The problem, if there is one, is not Robida's. It is ours. There is no reason why science fiction cannot sometimes be literally as well as metaphorically true. Moreover, we have been unduly reluctant to grant Robida, and science fiction, the possibility of occasionally combining genres that are usually regarded as incompatible. But in the best French tradition of rational paradox, Robida managed a rare feat, appropriately heralding our postmodern counterpart of the world that he imagines: *Le Vingtième siècle* adapts the genres of futuristic utopia, futuristic dystopia, and scientific adventure pioneered by Mercier, Souvestre, and Verne—the early masters of French science fiction—to combine utopia with dystopia by simultaneously showing the terrible shortcomings and the irresistible attractiveness of a world transformed by technology.

4

America: Technophobia

The arts and inventions of each period are only its costume and
do not invigorate men. The harm of the improved machinery may
compensate its good.

Ralph Waldo Emerson, "Self-Reliance"

Edgar Allan Poe: The Visionary Tradition

America's romance with technology has produced remarkably
diverse symbols ranging from the Promethean figure of
Benjamin Franklin flying his kite during a thunderstorm and
thus capturing celestial fire for humanity's benefit to the apocalyptic image of a mushroom cloud towering over Hiroshima as a
foretaste, perhaps, of humanity's end. Between these sublime
extremes equally varied and sometimes even ridiculous artifacts
have also been prominent in and outside literature as emblems
of America's utopian, dystopian, and merely quotidian applications of technology: Hawk-eye's deadly long rifle; the Bowie
knife; the Colt revolver; the iron horse displacing alike buffalo
and Indians; the *Pequod*'s harpoons, whale boats, and rendering
vats; the *Monitor* and the *Merrimack*; the telephone; Theodore

Roosevelt's Great White Fleet; the Golden Gate; the Empire State Building; Charles Lindbergh's *Spirit of St. Louis*; the flying fortress; the Mickey Mouse watch; Neil Armstrong's moon walk; the Star Ship *Enterprise*; the space shuttle *Enterprise*; and William Gibson's cyberspace. Much of America's history, including many of its best and worst moments, is encapsulated in such images of its technological artifacts and dreams. Every reader can add to the list. At striking variance from it is Edgar Allan Poe's (1809–49) most memorable contribution to our imagery of technology, in "The Pit and the Pendulum."

The horrifying razor-sharp pendulum inexorably descending to slice apart a man condemned by the Spanish Inquisition is described by its intended victim as "this machine."[1] It is Poe's archetypal emblem of human relationship to machinery. Its bleak meaning is unmistakable: the machines are our tormentors, not our saviors. It turns attention to the European past, not the American future. It is unforgettable. Its closest rival among Poe's tales is the even more primitive technology of trowel, mortar, and building stone used to bury Fortunato alive in "The Cask of Amontillado." His final despairing cry ("For the love of God, Montressor!") only serves to make more chilling the narrator's matter-of-fact concluding description of ancient technology applied to yet another sadistic new use: "I forced the last stone into its position; I plastered it up" (*Tales*, 518). The technology of these stories is so old-fashioned that on a casual first reading it hardly registers *as* technology, serving instead to create an unconscious aversion by association with its misapplication. The aversion is all the more powerful for being subliminal. Poe's more explicit science fictional encounters with machinery have nothing like the evocative force of the murderous technology at the heart of his best tales of pure horror. There is in common, however, a negative attitude.

The features of ballooning described with convincing verisimilitude in "The Balloon Hoax" serve no more positive purpose than to set up contemporary readers for the pratfall of discovering that they have been duped: no such transatlantic aerial voyage as is described in this phony news item had yet taken place. Their eagerness for a technological triumph has only made them foolishly gullible. Such faith in technology is exposed as a departure from reason and reality. Poe's implausible account of a bizarre lunar voyage via balloon in "The Unparalleled Adventure of One Hans Pfaall" is framed in such farcical tones as to under-cut serious appreciation of its nicely elaborated concern with views of the earth from outer space. Despite some attention to details of twenty-ninth-century dirigible construction and use in "Mellonta Tauta," the balloon *Skylark* on which the narrator trav-els remains a rather vague, unappealing object, as do the other balloons that share its unfriendly sky. One of them passing dan-gerously close above trailing a line that collides with the *Skylark* ominously seems to Poe's narrator "like an immense bird of prey about to pounce upon us and carry us off in its claws."[2] In Poe's future of sluggish technological advance his *Skylark* and its sister ships, although made of sturdier material than the silk of early balloons and capable of speeds approaching 100 miles per hour, still feature as standard equipment the drag rope familiar to nineteenth-century balloonists. By starting "Mellonta Tauta" (whose title is a Greek phrase from Sophocles's *Antigone* mean-ing "these things are in the future") with the date 1 April 2848, Poe invites more attention to the mood of April Fool's Day with its expectation of hoaxes than to the possibilities of serious fore-cast. Insofar as the tone shifts from comedy to thoughtful extrap-olation it is also a shift toward association of advanced aerial technology with a dystopian future, thus criticizing nineteenth-century optimism about the moral benefits of mechanical progress.

When the *Skylark*'s drag rope accidentally knocks overboard a passenger "from one of the small magnetic propellers that swarm in ocean below" the man "of course, was not permitted to get on board again, and was soon out of sight, he and his life-preserver" (*PSF*, 312). In response to this callous abandonment Poe's twenty-ninth-century female narrator merely rejoices to "live in an age so enlightened that no such a thing as an individ-ual is supposed to exist. It is the mass for which the true Humanity cares" (*PSF*, 311). Musing later with amazement at the centuries during which war and pestilence were thought calami-ties, Poe's narrator wonders how primitive people could be "so blind as not to perceive that the destruction of a myriad of indi-viduals is only so much positive advantage to the mass!" (*PSF*, 312). Moreover the narrator, who professes to write "altogether" for her own "amusement" heedless of whether anyone will actually read her account although it takes the form of a letter to a friend, is equally indifferent to her own imminent destruction, finally noting without emotion that she must close because—for no apparent reason—"the balloon has collapsed, and we shall have a tumble into the sea" (*PSF*, 322). Here unreliable technology is the sign of an ethically unreliable society. Poe's derisive emblem of the future is a collapsing balloon.

In several other works Poe takes up material that we now think of as science fictional but usually without either discarding his penchant for Gothic horror or transmuting it effectively into other modes. "Eureka: An Essay on the Material and Spiritual Universe" is precisely what its title proclaims: an essay in speculative science. As such it is, like many another in the nineteenth century, of considerable interest. But the pleasures of story are absent. It is science without fiction except in the abstract sense in which all theories may be considered (nonnarrative) fictions. The aesthetics of such fictionalizing are those of science itself, not science fiction. Poe employs the science of mesmerism—but mingled ambiguously with the supernatural—as a focus of speculation, narrative suspense, and horrific effects in "A Tale of the Ragged Mountains," "Mesmeric Revelation," and "The Facts in the Case of M. Valdemar." The latter two finally rivet attention more on corpses than concepts. In "A Descent into the Maelström," Poe is more concerned with the psychology of fear than with either a puzzling natural phenomenon of the ocean or ways in which it might be used (as Verne went on to do) as a trope for larger issues. "The Conversation of Eiros and Charmion" describes from a fantastic postmortem perspective, and in under six pages, a comet strike that ends human life on earth. This topic demands a wider canvas: apocalypse is not the best subject for a miniaturist. Here Poe's genius for compression falters.

"Some Words with a Mummy" takes up Jane Webb's idea of galvanic resurrection in so farcical a manner as to make this story more a weak parody of its own genre than an effective vehicle for Poe's message—conveyed here by a resurrected mummy dubiously named "Allamistakeo"—that the nineteenth century is in no way an improvement over life in the age of the Pharaohs. The most impressive feats of modern technology, Allamistakeo insists, were anticipated or exceeded in ancient Egypt. Given some chapters from the transcendentalist quarterly *Dial* (edited by Emerson and others) on "something which is not very clear, but which the Bostonians call the Great Movement or Progress," the mummy retorts "that Great Movements were awfully common things in his day, and as for Progress it was at one time quite a nuisance, but it never progressed" (*PSF*, 168–69). Allamistakeo's most dismaying news is that the ancient world saw a declaration of independence by thirteen Egyptian provinces determined "to be free, and so set a magnificent example to the rest of mankind" but whose experiment in democracy ended "in the consolidation of the thirteen states, with some fifteen or twenty others, in the most odious and insupportable despotism that ever was heard of upon the face of the earth"—a tyranny ruled by "*Mob*" (*PSF*, 169). After hearing the mummy's report Poe's narrator, who is "heartily sick of this life and of the nineteenth century in general," resolves to emulate Allamistakeo by getting "embalmed for a couple of hundred years" (*PSF*, 170). The death wish so prominent in Poe's fiction is here presented comically, as is his aversion to technology. Less amusing is Poe's satiric association of democracy and technology as equally contemptible features of the modern world.

Bruce Franklin is right to brand Poe's outlook as "essentially anti-scientific and downright escapist" because "despite all his dabbling with scientific and technologial speculation . . . he preferred to look away from physical and social reality—the actual wonders and dangers of nineteenth-century experimental science and the actual horrors and perversions of the slave system he supported—toward his own illusory theories, unworkable inventions, and imagined terrors."[3] In the first half of the twentieth century Poe was widely accepted as of equal status with Verne and Wells as a founder of science fiction, thanks especially to Hugo Gernsback's promotional efforts on Poe's behalf in *Amazing Stories*, to his popularity in France, and to the ascendancy of short stories. But commentators after 1950 with an eye on later developments have been less inclined to give him so much credit while nevertheless unable to brick him up safely out of sight in a tomb reserved for the genres of horror.

Kingsley Amis found "some mention of Poe . . . sadly difficult to avoid" but locates his significance mainly in the fact "that Verne learnt more from Poe than from any other writer."[4] This exaggerates Verne's debt. Although he was certainly inspired by Poe among others to focus on the psychology of bizarre situations (including balloon flights) in strange locales, Verne's fiction has closer affinities with writing more centered on realism and rationalism. If we must have a single archetype for him, we do better to accept Darko Suvin's perceptive choice of Defoe because of Verne's penchant for the plot structure of the Robinsonade and because "as in *Robinson Crusoe*, Verne's great model, his characters are constantly menaced by the doom of dehumanizing solitude on their individual psychic islands."[5] Brian Aldiss concedes Poe's importance as a source of techniques for enhancing awe and wonder by hinting at unknowable, irrational facts lurking behind the apparently comprehensible phenomena of nature described by science, but he insists too that "far from being the Father of Science Fiction, this genius bodged it when he confronted its themes directly. Yet he brought off some of its best effects, more or less when looking the other way."[6] Aldiss suggests that Poe's ultimate contribution was perfection of the short story as an effective medium because shorter forms are most congenial to science fiction. This truth has been at once confirmed and obscured since the 1960s by commercial market pressures that have given long science fiction novels (often with interminable sequels) economic though seldom aesthetic ascendancy over short story anthologies.[7] In the last part of the twentieth century science fiction's chronic (but not hereditary) disease has been elephantiasis. From this at least Poe did not suffer.

Bruce Franklin relegates Poe to a juvenile library appealing to the perennially immature: "Poe, then, may be the father not of science fiction but rather of what is so often associated with the term science fiction—fiction which popularizes science for boys and girls of all ages while giving them the creeps" (*FP*, 98). David Ketterer concludes that although "no single work of Poe's qualifies as what is generally understood as 'straight' science fiction" everything Poe wrote "can be regarded as marginally science-fictional" because "in providing a visionary reality out of space and time with a science-fictional rationale, Poe inaugurated that visionary tradition of science fiction that owes nothing to Jules Verne but that includes many of the masterpieces of the genre."[8] This rightly links Poe to writers perceived as within, if sometimes just barely within, the now blurring boundaries separating science fiction from fantasy, but it fails to acknowledge sufficiently the visionary qualities of Verne's fiction in which science is so often enlisted in the service of romantic symbolism. Darko Suvin comes closer to identifying Poe's affinity with Vernian as well as other modes of science fiction by noting somewhat regretfully that "Poe's influence has been immense in both Anglo-American and French SF (the latter has yet to recover from it)" because "though his ideology and time-horizon tend to horror-fantasy, the pioneering incompleteness of his work provided SF too with a wealth of hints for fusing the rational with the symbolical" (Suvin, 143). The irony of Poe's strong technophobia is that it impelled him to experiment with forms of fantasy that taught his successors how to enhance the suggestive power of all science fiction, whether employed to advocate or attack technology. And for a century after Poe's death in 1849 technology found more advocates than enemies in America.

Edward Bellamy: Looking Backward: 2000–1887

Nowhere in nineteenth-century science fiction is America's infatuation with technology more influentially expressed than in Edward Bellamy's *Looking Backward: 2000–1887* (1888). By 1900 this sketch of Boston in the year 2000 had sold by the millions, been translated into more than twenty languages, and had achieved an impact on social thought that has often been ranked as second only to Karl Marx's *Das Kapital* (1867). Bellamy indeed touched a similar chord in giving narrative shape to the Marxist dream of a society governed by the principle, "From everyone according to his faculties, to everyone according to his needs." Bellamy clubs were formed throughout America to discuss his ideas, which led also to formation of a political party, the Nationalists, to push for their implementation. In response to *Looking Backward* more than fifty related utopias were written by 1900, some in agreement, many in opposition to its millennial vision of a future America purged by the year 2000 of all the poverty, disease, and wasted lives caused, Bellamy suggests in *Looking Backward*, by private capitalism with "its tendency toward monopolies"; yet paradoxically his ideal America is "organized as the one great business corporation in which all other corporations were absorbed . . . the one capitalist in place of all other capitalists, the sole employer, the final monopoly in which all previous and lesser monopolies were swallowed up."[9] The most famous of the counterutopias written in immediate response to *Looking Backward* is William Morris's *News from Nowhere*, published in England in 1890. Its cloying pastoral vision of a less centralized and mechanized future is offered as an alternative to what Morris found most appalling in *Looking Backward*: "a machine life is the best which Bellamy can imagine for us on all sides; it is not to be wondered at then that his only idea of making labour tolerable is to decrease the amount of it by means of fresh and ever fresh developments of machinery."[10]

This frequently echoed complaint distorts Bellamy's emphasis on machines. But Morris's readiness to misread *Looking Backward* on this topic epitomizes a striking difference between preponderant American belief in the utopian possibilities of technology and a prevailing English suspicion of its dangers. Within science fiction that distrust was most memorably expressed by H. G. Wells's vivid account of Martian war machines destroying human civilization.[11] A telling American response to *The War of the Worlds* is Garrett P. Serviss's unauthorized sequel, *Edison's Conquest of Mars*. In this classic exemplar of science fiction's worst strain of xenophobic jingoism, serialized in the January and February, 1898, issues of the *New York Evening Journal* just before outbreak of the Spanish-American War in April of that year, Thomas Alva Edison's legendary status as archetypal American scientific genius becomes the foundation of a tale in which Edison first invents antigravity spaceships and disintegrator weapons and then organizes and leads an expedition to defeat the Martians on their planet while also liberating a beautiful captive Earthwoman named Aina and pausing to explore the moon en route. Like Villiers de l'Isle-Adam, Serviss fastens on the technological possibilities symbolized by Edison, but he does so in ways that point neither toward the philosophical concerns of *Tomorrow's Eve* nor toward serious consideration of what present and future technology may actually import for humanity. Instead Serviss paves the way for space opera of the kind most widely popularized by the Martian fantasies that Edgar Rice Burroughs initiated in 1917 with his best-seller *A Princess of Mars*.

Far from appropriating Edison for the mythology of science fiction to interrogate the cogito, as Villiers had done in the best Cartesian tradition, *Edison's Conquest of Mars* proceeds in the worst American vein of extroversion to abolish introspection by exploiting and expanding Edison's legend for what has been well described as "mindless glorification of the cults of progress, empire, individualism, and technology."[12]

Though Serviss represents the most hawkish wing of American technophilia, Bellamy must be counted among its doves. Despite his affirmation of advanced technology as the sine qua non of utopia, *Looking Backward* envisions a world whose vital force is not technology itself, nor empire, nor what Bellamy denounces as "excessive individualism," but "the brotherhood of man" fostered by a state capitalism that has eliminated warfare and armies along with political parties, lawyers, taxation, money (replaced by "credit cards"), serious crime, jails, and the need for a large police force (*LB*, 57, 83, 111). The role of technology in Bellamy's future, though crucial, is in fact much less dominating or sinister than hostile critics of *Looking Backward* like William Morris suggest.

The ultimate purpose of Bellamy's twenty-first-century gadgetry is to liberate people for retirement at age 45 so they can, as that century's spokesman Doctor Leete explains, fully devote themselves "to the higher exercise of our faculties, the intellectual and spiritual enjoyments and pursuits, which alone mean life" (*LB*, 148). Morris was right to see that *Looking Backward* is no paean to the dignity of labor. Doctor Leete dismisses work necessary to secure "the means of a comfortable physical existence" as "by no means . . . the most important, the most interesting, or the most dignified employment of our powers" (*LB*, 148). Bellamy's denigration of labor was aimed, however, neither at intellectual pursuits—authorship, for example, is encouraged in his future— nor at the idealized work of artisans so dear to Morris and those who in his pre-Raphaelite vein romanticize the cultivation of arts and crafts. Bellamy only targets those who applied social Darwinism to justify the actual horrors of industrialized sweatshops serving mainly to enrich a handful of capitalists and managers. Unlike the heartless industrialism whose social consequences are portrayed so well in the novels of Dickens, which are alluded to in *Looking Backward* (no less than in *News from*

Nowhere) as the best account of nineteenth-century deficiencies, the technology of Bellamy's future is applied to make life both easier and more spiritually rewarding even before retirement.

There are public kitchens and laundries to eliminate major items of household drudgery. Public shops make and mend clothing so no one has to do this at home. Bellamy plugs in nineteenth-century science fiction's unfailing source of futuristic power: "Electricity, of course, takes the place of all fires and lighting" (*LB*, 102). Anticipating the dictum that less is more, houses are scaled down to the needs of their inhabitants. A telephone broadcasting system provides a wide selection of music for private listening 24 hours per day, thus bringing culture to everyone, not just (as in the nineteenth century) those with enough leisure and money to attend concerts. On Sundays there is a choice among broadcast sermons (of which a sample is provided to edify readers). But all this has been not been achieved merely as an inevitable consequence or extension of what Bellamy describes as "an age of steam and telegraphs and the gigantic scale of its enterprises" (*LB*, 65). It is the other way around. Technological innovation liberating individuals to pursue their personal development has been spurred by *prior* social reform equalizing all citizens as fellow workers for the nation's benefit, thus eliminating the "boundless supply of serfs on whom you could impose all sorts of painful and disagreeable tasks. . . . This fact has given a prodigious impulse to labor-saving inventions in all sorts of industry" (*LB*, 102). The age of steam and telegraphs has made leveling social reform more possible as well as more desirable than ever before. The grand result is a "an era of mechanical invention, scientific discovery, art, musical and literary productiveness to which no previous age of the world offers anything comparable" (*LB*, 128).

Bellamy's characterization of this prodigious artistic no less than technological and scientific progress as a development "of which the outburst of the medieval Renaissance offers a suggestion but faint indeed" (*LB*, 128) doubtless further annoyed Morris, who proposed for humanity's model no such future as Bellamy's but an idealized fourteenth century that as a result of deliberate scaling back has even less advanced technology than the real fourteenth century, except for incongruous "force barges" plying the Thames. Bellamy's vision differs most significantly in explicitly putting art, music, and literature on the same plane with science and "mechanical invention." In *Looking Backward* there is no debilitating subordination of the arts to technology—or vice versa.

Their equality in Bellamy's scheme must be understood to appreciate why *Looking Backward* figures so prominently among those 25 "technological utopias" identified by Howard P. Segal as published between 1880 and 1930 in the United States offering pictures of a utopian future in which "domestication of both technology and nature would lead to a resolution of the allegedly permanent tension between the industrial and the agrarian order, or the machine and the garden, which Leo Marx has said lies at the heart of the American experience." Segal notes that these technological utopias are marked not only by "the introduction of new tools and machines" but equally by modeling on them of "institutions, values, and culture."[13] In *Looking Backward*, however, Bellamy's future America is not modeled directly on any one machine or group of machines, but on a social entity described (in a familiar Enlightenment metaphor) as machine-like: the army. There is an "industrial army" in which all the citizens of Bellamy's twenty-first century are enlisted to do the country's work. As in the combat armies on which it is modeled there are ranks. Its discipline is severe: "A man able to duty, and persistently refusing, is sentenced to solitary imprisonment on bread and water till he consents" (*LB*, 107). As a step toward equality of the sexes there is a women's army, an "allied force" with its own female general (*LB*, 185). Bellamy gives women not the modest room of one's own that Virginia Woolf later proposed but, more grandiosely, "a world of their own" where they can have the satisfactions of a career on their terms without any "unnatural rivalry with men" (*LB*, 186). Maternity leave is available. Doctor Leete enthusiastically compares this core institution of his age with "such a fighting machine, for example, as the German army in the time of Von Moltke" (*LB*, 177). In a comparison probably a good deal more appealing for Bellamy's American readers then and certainly now, his protagonist Julian West imagines a Union regiment on parade as a "tremendous engine" and wonders how people of his day could "fail to compare the scientific manner in which the nation went to war with the unscientific manner in which it went to work" (*LB*, 225).

Looking Backward proposes mobilizing for peace with the same machinelike efficiency used to mobilize Northern armies for combat in the 1860s.

Haunting Bellamy's utopia are memories of the Civil War, surely for all the nobility of its success in saving the Union and emancipating slaves also a paradigm of modern technology's unprecedented ferocity. But Bellamy focuses on the Union army's constructive achievements, using the machine metaphor as a further source of positive connotations for his industrial army and its world on the assumption that readers will be favorably disposed to whatever may be compared in point of efficiency with modern machinery—if applied solely to beneficent purposes. It is an irony of history that those who now look back from a post-Hiroshima perspective are often far more strongly impelled than William Morris ever was to literalize what Bellamy intended merely as a familiar organizing trope comparing society with machinery, and therefore to see in *Looking Backward* only what David Ketterer dismisses as "a dystopian society in which the citizens have evolved, or rather devolved, into machines" (Ketterer, 113).

Bellamy's failure to achieve a consensus among readers about whether his future is desirable or undesirable, utopian or dystopian, truly human or merely mechanistic, is to some extent a feature of utopias as a genre from the slyly satiric ambiguities of Sir Thomas More's *Utopia* to the explicitly ambiguous utopias of the twentieth century such as Ursula K. Le Guin's masterpiece *The Dispossessed* (1974). All utopias invite readers to take stock of their own attitudes toward both their actual world and the one depicted. The best utopias, arguably, are those which provoke the most intense reaction, whether positive or negative, by way of a heuristic for action in the real world.[14] Insofar as the debates over *Looking Backward* reflect such intensity of response, whether in agreement or disagreement, they are another measure of its success in stimulating engagement with the question of how technology does or should shape our lives. But much of the persistent misunderstanding of its proposals on the role of technology stems from Bellamy's inability to show vividly the superiority or even the existence of that art, music, and literature that we are assured abound alongside mechanical inventions in his twenty-first century. Such abstract assurances have little persuasive force. They quickly fade out of the reader's memory.

It is a measure of Bellamy's contribution to science fiction that what stays in mind alongside his sketch of a future America is Julian West's Crusoe-like problem of being stranded in that distant time. His difficulties are dramatic surrogates for those of readers struggling to come to terms with Bellamy's vision. West achieves a solution (denied to readers though enhancing their interest in his story) that is both erotic and ideological, as he falls in love with an inhabitant of the future while also coming to accept, not without difficulty, its social philosophy. After being accidentally left in a mesmeric trance for 113 years for reasons that are given a sufficient if rather strained degree of plausibility according to prevailing fictive conventions, he is aroused and must adjust to life in what for him (as for readers) is the strange world of Boston in the year 2000.

Bellamy follows the tedious pattern of traditional utopias by providing conversation after conversation between his protagonist and an older resident of the utopian community (Doctor Leete) who describes in excruciating detail its social arrangements and virtues. By placing his utopia in imaginary future time but in a real place Bellamy imitates with more success the model of uchronic utopia provided in 1771 by Louis-Sébastien Mercier's *L'An 2440*, although reversing one aspect of this model by giving Julian West at the end a nightmare of returning to the ghastly nineteenth century from which he wakes with relief to find that he really and permanently is in the twenty-first century. Within the fiction his trip ahead is given a solidity denied to those which are dismissed at the end as mere dreams from which the narrator is finally aroused, like Mercier, to the bitter realities of his own era. The use of mesmerism as an agent of time travel instead of dream vision in the manner of Mercier or slumber in the manner of Rip Van Winkle brings *Looking Backward* away from fantasy into the realm of science fiction, as does to an even greater degree Bellamy's attempt to extrapolate from nineteenth-century technological and social realities a possible if unlikely future that can serve as an invitation for readers to reassess the nature and directions of their present society. Bellamy makes his future seem more real than Mercier's by virtue of West's permanent residence in it as the reader's surrogate, and of course more provocative of cognitive estrangement than Rip Van Winkle's by virtue of more significant differences from the past. Bellamy's greatest departure from utopian precedent is in the amount of text devoted to elaborating Julian West's psychological response to what for him is the jarring experience and for readers the intriguing one of going to sleep in one world and waking "with no sense of any lapse of time" into another (*LB*, 79).

West first suffers a complete dissolution of identity during which he is unable to distinguish himself "from pure being." After struggling back to awareness of selfhood as a distinct personality there follows an interval in which he feels himself to be somehow "two persons" at once living with a "double" identity, and a more protracted interval in which as he walks around the twenty-first-century city images of the old and new Boston clash in a kind of unstable psychological palimpsest "so that it was first one and then the other which seemed the more unreal" (*LB*, 77–79). Such passages now seem less an echo of Poe than anticipations of Philip K. Dick. There accumulates for West "a horror of strangeness" so acute "as to produce actual nausea" (*LB*, 80). Here Bellamy anticipates with almost equivalent emotional though not philosophical force that existential nausea experienced farther in the future by H. G. Wells's Time Traveller. By so often taking readers into West's tormented mind, Bellamy points to ways in which the ideological concerns of science fiction can be effectively merged with the compelling dramatic interests of the psychological novel.

Darko Suvin stresses Bellamy's integration of ideology and psychology in *Looking Backward* by noting (without dwelling upon the preponderance of lectures by Doctor Leete) that "its plot is, in fact, Julian's change of identity" from nineteenth- to twenty-first-century citizen: "the construction of a social system for the reader is also the reconstruction of the hero" (Suvin, 174). This is true. A problem, however, is that the inner and outer drama of Bellamy's plot is overshadowed by one-sided dialogue as Doctor Leete relentlessly explains every facet of twenty-first-century life. Readers will too often feel that they are locked in a sociology lecture hall where the bell never rings. Bellamy's considerable novelization of utopia nevertheless provides what Peter Fitting describes as "a significant transformation in the construction of the reader: from the addressee in a philosophic dialogue who is persuaded through reasoned presentation, as in Thomas More's *Utopia*, to an emotional and experiential involvement with a fictional character whose changing attitudes and feelings are designed to increase the reader's own interest and concern."[15] As a milestone in American science fiction *Looking Backward*, despite its longueurs, is finally notable not only for its eloquent affirmation that technology may serve instead of subverting humane purposes, but also for its attempt to combine the stasis of utopia with the action of story.

Mark Twain: A Connecticut Yankee in King Arthur's Court

Mark Twain filled *A Connecticut Yankee in King Arthur's Court* (1889) with enough action for several stories, and surrounded it with story. Its action centers on the adventures of Hank Morgan, superintendent of the Colt arms-factory in Hartford, who finds himself transported to Arthurian England, which he unsuccessfully attempts to industrialize and democratize, and then back again to the nineteenth century. On arrival in Camelot, Morgan is imprisoned and nearly burnt at the stake as a suspicious stranger, but uses foreknowledge of an eclipse to save himself by persuading the natives that he is a great magician who controls the sun. This feat earns him promotion (as "Sir Boss") over his rival Merlin, who is further humiliated when his tower is blown up during a thunderstorm by a charge of blasting powder that Morgan secretly concocts and wires up to a lightning rod after announcing that he will again demonstrate his superiority as a magician. Later, by using his engineering expertise to restore a defective well venerated by monks in the Valley of Holiness (while also impressing the locals and visiting pilgrims with a fireworks display), Morgan yet again bests Merlin at what is taken for magic but is actually another application of nineteenth-century technological know-how. After his initial triumphs Morgan exuberantly (but prematurely) concludes that "every time the magic of fol-de-rol tried conclusions with the magic of science, the magic of fol-de-rol got left."[16] Having thus secured a position second only to the king himself, Morgan then sets about introducing into Arthur's realm what the title of chapter 10 calls the "Beginnings of Civilization": such (then) futuristic novelties as printed books, newspapers, bicycles, railroads, steamships, "the telegraph, the telephone, the phonograph, the type-writer, the sewing machine, and all the thousand willing and handy servants of steam and electricity" (CY, 397). To complement these technological advances Morgan manages (for a while) to abolish slavery and render all men equal before the law as a prelude to what he hopes will be eventual replacement of monarchy by a democratically elected government and replacement of England's established Roman Catholic Church by religious toleration in an American-style system of competing Protestant sects whose number will prevent any one of them from hindering religious freedom or achieving political control, "it being my conviction," he explains, "that any Established church is an established crime, an established slave-pen . . . an enemy to human liberty" (CY, 139, 161). He also introduces schools, colleges, military academies, a patent office, American-style currency, a stock exchange, factories, advertising campaigns to popularize what the factories produce (especially soap and toothpaste), and as a crowning touch for his new civilization, baseball teams.

While masterminding all this, Morgan is involved too in tournaments that he wins by arming himself with a lasso and revolvers instead of lance, sword, and shield. He plays the game by his own rules, seeing himself as "the champion of hard, unsentimental common-sense and reason . . . entering the lists to either destroy knight-errantry or be its victim" (CY, 384). He wants eventually to bring down the aristocracy along with monarchy and the Church. Meanwhile, partly to get to know the country and partly to humor court customs, he takes time off for an old-style excursion of knight-errantry (in full and uncomfortable armor) to help a damsel in distress, Demoiselle Alisande la Carteloise, whom he nicknames Sandy and later marries. The object of their quest is to rescue some imprisoned nobility, who turn out to be a herd of swine—victims of enchantment, Sandy insists. Twain's symbolism in this part makes up in effective comedy what it lacks in subtlety (augmented, as throughout, by Daniel Carter Beard's brilliant illustrations, here most prominently a delicious picture of Queen Victoria metamorphosed into a pig, "the troublesomest old Sow of the lot"). Morgan and King Arthur make an incognito inspection trip around Britain that nearly ends in disaster when they are mistaken for dangerous commoners, enslaved, mistreated, condemned to death for trying to escape, and rescued just in the nick of time at the foot of the gallows by Sir Launcelot leading a cavalry charge of "five hundred mailed and belted knights on bicycles" (*CY*, 379). Each of these episodes provides almost enough material for a novel. Strung together they parody medieval romances and modern adventure stories while also providing many of their excitements and giving *A Connecticut Yankee* some of the nostalgic appeal of picaresque fiction. Twain's mixture of high adventure, low comedy, fierce satire, and anachronistic utopian tinkering with medieval society ends on a tragic note when all Morgan's efforts to use technology as a basis for democracy collapse in a final hideous battle against forces of the old order, where the Yankee's nineteenth-century weapons bring no victory for reason or democracy but only appalling slaughter.

The story that surrounds Hank Morgan's activities—and Twain's text—is Sir Thomas Malory's *Morte Darthur*, published in 1485 by William Caxton using England's first printing press. This magnificent collaboration of a writer and a technician who was also on occasion a writer is in turn surrounded by all the Matter of Britain: the myriad tellings and retellings throughout the Middle Ages of how Camelot rose and fell. Malory, like Twain after him, could fit his tale to the template of a familiar basic plot that starts with comedy as young Arthur becomes king and ends with tragedy as moral blindness on all sides destroys the noble Order of the Round Table that he tries to establish as a civilizing force. It was also possible to draw on a familiar cast of characters who were expected to turn up with interesting variations as well as familiar features in particular versions: Arthur, Guenever, Mordred, Morgan le Fay, Merlin, Launcelot, Gawain, Galahad, and the rest. The many-faceted Arthurian myth so fundamental not only to English and French literature but to the articulation of ethical aspirations in Western civilization, and so rich in meanings, is above all—as it is also in Twain's version—the story of a failed attempt to create a perfect society. It is a tale of utopia thrice lost: lost because always out of reach in the past, lost because never fully achieved, and lost too outside time because Arthur's reign is placed back in a legendary past that never was. We couldn't get there from here even if we had a time machine.

Camelot has always been in mythic, not historical, time. Even according to the vague standards of historicity accepted by medieval writers of Arthurian romance, King Arthur is supposed to have existed not in any chronologically verifiable relationship to their own present but back in some indeterminate good old days, a "once upon a time" long ago if not far away, a golden age that somehow turned into our leaden present after the end of Camelot. Medieval historians are hardly more precise. Thus Twain's Connecticut Yankee does not simply travel backward in time from his starting point in 1879 to a destination in our past, even though Twain's text specifies Hank Morgan's temporal terminus ad quem as June A.D. 528. He travels from history to myth. He is sent altogether outside calendric time into an imaginary universe that partly resembles ours and whose chronology can be assigned dates running parallel to those in the calendar of real time, but that is free from the constraints of actual history. Twain sends his (imaginary) Yankee not from his (real) readers' present to a medieval past like the one that historians describe, but from the world of nineteenth-century fiction to a world inspired by Malory's *Morte Darthur*. These home truths are worth laboring because to overlook them, as too many of Twain's critics do, is to misunderstand the remarkable originality of *A Connecticut Yankee in King Arthur's Court*, its genre, its degree of coherence, and its extraordinary vitality as an archetype for science fiction's subgenre of time travel stories.

Only recently has it been recognized that *A Connecticut Yankee in King Arthur's Court* is the first story of travel to and from the past. This motif does not occur in previous literature or folklore. Nor do attempts like the Yankee's to meddle with the past in order to change it. Before Twain the present only encounters an immutable past in the form of ruins, relics, monuments, histories, and magical manifestations of earlier days as when Doctor Faustus conjures up Helen of Troy.[17] The past may tamper with the present as in Gothic tales of ghosts clamoring for or enacting retribution—and it is indeed a main purpose of Gothic fiction to dramatize various ways in which the past maintains an icy grip on the present.[18] But no one before Twain imagined a figure from the present going back to alter the past.

By the late nineteenth century, as I have noted in previous chapters, there was ample precedent for tales set in future time and for one-way travel to the future in the manner of Julian West or Rip Van Winkle. The latter had folkloristic antecedents in such legends as the tale of the Seven Sleepers of Ephesus and even in accounts of the enchanted sleep from which Arthur, whom Malory calls *Rex quondam Rex que futurus* (the once and future king), will one day awake to rule again. The ancient device of dream vision provided a form that could be adapted to futuristic fiction as Mercier did in *L'An 2440* without greatly disrupting verisimilitude because narrated future experiences turn out to have been only a dream (and in a dream anything can happen). Hank Morgan's journey to the past, like Julian West's one-way trip to the future, is presented as no dream but something that really happened to him. The closest approach to tales of travel to the past were historical novels of the kind popularized by Sir Walter Scott and alternative histories of the kind inaugurated by Louis Geoffroy, but neither of these forms makes an explicit leap to projection of a fictive character from the reader's present into the depicted actual or alternative past. In them it is only readers who are brought close to the past, though merely as external spectators seeing it from outside without any power to influence the (fictive) ancient events of which they read. It is unlikely that Geoffroy's seldom-imitated *Napoleon and the Conquest of the World* was known to Twain, although certainly historical novels were a stimulus to his imagination, as they were in other ways to those who wrote futuristic fiction. One purpose of *A Connecticut Yankee in King Arthur's Court* is to debunk romanticized accounts of an idealized past. Morgan finds himself in an age whose few appealing moments of chivalric pageantry and genuine heroism are overshadowed by squalor, brutality, ignorance, and superstition.

It does not diminish Twain's originality to remark that it is *Robinson Crusoe* even more than Arthurian legend that serves as structural archetype for *A Connecticut Yankee*. When Hank Morgan first grasps that he has been transported from the comforts of his nineteenth-century United States to a disagreeably primitive place and time without electricity, gaslight, candles, window glass, newspapers, books, pens, paper, ink, or even sugar, coffee, tea, and tobacco, he recalls the great precedent for both his predicament and its amelioration: "I saw that I was just another Robinson Crusoe cast away on an uninhabited island, with no society but some more or less tame animals, and if I wanted to make life bearable I must do as he did—invent, contrive, create, reorganize things, set brains and hand to work, and keep them busy" (*CY*, 54). Morgan is tragically mistaken to think so patronizingly of the earlier people as tame or at least tamable but inferior creatures, "just like so many children" as he puts it elsewhere (*CY*, 30). He underestimates both the attractions and the dangers of the past. But he is right to compare himself with Crusoe (who also misunderstood the dangers of his primitive environment), and in so doing he provides a hint (from Twain) about how to read his story, how to locate it generically. Bud Foote comments that "All tales of temporal stranding are *robinsonades*. . . . Just as Defoe created a whole new subspecies of fiction with *Robinson Crusoe*, a hymn to rugged individualism and the processes of technology, so among Twain's many accomplishments must be numbered the adaptation of that subspecies to the temporal sphere."[19] In his excellent analysis of *A Connecticut Yankee* as a paradigm for understanding later varieties of time travel stories of which it is the progenitor, Foote also addresses the difficult questions of why the idea of travel to the past should have occurred first in late-nineteenth-century America, and why such an impossibility as time travel is so much a staple of science fiction from Twain forward rather than a hallmark of fantasy.

Americans, Foote reminds us, were and are more likely than Europeans to equate geography with time, and thus spatial with temporal travel, because in the New World, especially during America's expansionist nineteenth century, the western frontier stands for the future whereas eastern states and Europe ("the old country") stand for the past. To travel west is to go toward a cultural future. To travel east is to go toward the cultural past. The further east one goes, the more one encounters old buildings and monuments and the greater their antiquity. Americans crossing the Atlantic eastward to Europe (as in Twain's *Innocents Abroad*, 1869) are also in effect visiting their collective past. In Europe, where past and present structures more often coexist rather evenly distributed despite local pockets more densely crowded with antiquities or altogether without them, there is no such pronounced sensation of temporal travel accompanying geographic movement. The nineteenth century was also marked by an expansion of tourism facilitated by new modes of rapid transport such as railroads and steamships. Imperialistic rather than touristic travel from developed to undeveloped lands for purposes of exploitation of technologically primitive natives was also a kind of trip from present to past and back again. Accompanying all these developments in nineteenth-century America with its rapid growth, westward movement of population, and expanding industrialization that outpaced that of Europe, where the industrial revolution had started in the eighteenth century, there was an acute awareness of technological change that could be experienced geographically in movement from countryside to city, and especially from the agrarian South to a far more urban and industrialized North. To look out of a train window or stand contemplating the shore from the deck of a riverboat on such a trip was in effect to see past give way to present or vice versa depending on the direction of one's journey. And as Foote also reminds us, Twain not only worked as a steamboat pilot traveling north and south on the Mississippi but had gone from brief service in the Confederacy (from which he deserted after two weeks) to live eventually in the Northeast after adventures in the far West. His life exemplifies American mobility. Dramatic industrialization during his lifetime also accentuated differences between the agrarian America of his childhood and the more urbanized America of his later years, that is, between past and present, thereby creating a sensation of having lived in two distinct eras. Foote suggests that the new ease as well as the very reversibility of trips through spaces representing strikingly different layers of cultural time led to Twain's conceit in *A Connecticut Yankee* of going backward and forward in time. There is no way of being sure what brings about such literary innovation, which usually involves multiple causes. But Foote's suggestion is bolstered by the fact that Hank Morgan also goes from Connecticut to England, so that his time travel, unlike Julian West's purely temporal movement from the Boston of 1887 to that of 2000, is displacement from west to east as well as from present to past. Certainly American equation of geographic space with cultural time, however it influenced Twain, would help prepare his readers for works like *A Connecticut Yankee*.

Twain's cavalier disregard of verisimilitude in accounting for Hank Morgan's time travel makes even more problematic the question of why *A Connecticut Yankee* stands as the archetype of an important branch of science fiction rather than fantasy. Morgan explains that after being bashed over the head with a crowbar during a fight at the Colt arms-factory he lost consciousness and came to in what he discovered to be Arthurian England, where he was quickly captured by a mounted knight in full armor, who turned out to be Arthur's Seneschal Sir Kay, and brought to Camelot. After the eventual disastrous collapse of Morgan's effort to industrialize and democratize the sixth-century England in which he is stuck, Merlin puts him into an enchanted sleep from which he wakes again in the nineteenth century, though still in England. Here he meets "M.T." during a tour of Warwick Castle, falls into conversation, and later gives M.T. a written autobiographical narrative, which forms *A Connecticut Yankee* except for its "Preface" signed Mark Twain and dated "Hartford, July 21, 1889"; a preliminary chapter entitled "A Word of Explanation" evidently by Twain describing the encounter in Warwick Castle; a "Postscript by Clarence" explaining Merlin's enchantment of Morgan; and a "Final P.S. by M.T." recounting Morgan's death. None of the framing material attempts any scientific explanation of his time travel, or even scientific patter of the kind H. G. Wells later supplied to augment the verisimilitude created by his idea of a machine that could (somehow) travel through time as others traveled through space. There is only Morgan's vague question to M.T., "You know about transmigration of souls, do you know about transposition of epochs—and bodies?" (CY, 2).

If one does not know about such temporal transpositions—and no one would since they were not a familiar theme of previous fiction or folklore—the enigma of Morgan's trip to the past is only made less susceptible to natural explanation by his question, which invites readers to fall back on prescientific notions of magic and hazy ideas about transmigration that do not quite fit, as there was no body waiting in the past to receive Morgan's spirit: he wakes up outside Camelot not only in his own person but (much to the amusement of locals) in his own nineteenth-century clothing. He has traveled physically, not just in mind or spirit. From a late-twentieth-century perspective informed by all the time travel stories of which *A Connecticut Yankee* is the ancestor, and especially in comparison with Wells's concern to put a veneer of scientific plausibility over the impossibility of time travel by invoking a machine, what stands out in Twain's pioneering effort is his almost belligerent toying with the issue of

verisimilitude on this point. He provides only enough speculation to make sure readers notice that an explanation is desirable,
although no satisfactory one is available. He then drops the matter to proceed with his story and expects readers to follow suit. *A
Connecticut Yankee* is nevertheless within the boundaries of science fiction, Foote rightly suggests, because it is so concerned to
juxtapose past and future: "If the central tension of science fiction may be described as past pulling against future (or rural
against urban; agricultural against industrial; the village against
the metropolis . . .), then *the literature of time travel to the past has a
place in science fiction, not because of any intrinsic plausibility, but
because its central tensions are the same tensions—and more nakedly
expressed—which generate the central energies of science fiction"*
(Foote, 83). It is the narrative presence of time travel, not the
means of achieving it, which is central to the emerging new
genre of science fiction.

Because we are so used to machines that do all manner of
things without external evidence of how exactly they do them,
Wells's device of a time machine provides an explanation of time
travel that is no more scientifically valid than the idea of bashing
someone over the head with a crowbar to initiate departure from
the present but that is nevertheless now far more acceptable as a
literary convention precisely because its spurious technological
air serves as a satisfactory *substitute* for valid explanations. Wells,
in turning to the future as an arena for speculation, brilliantly
established a convention that largely eliminated distracting questions about the actual possibility of time travel (although many
fine stories have dealt with this issue and its paradoxes). Twain
in turning to the past as an arena for exploring the consequences
of industrialization provided a new setting allowing better
engagement of science fiction with history. At their best subsequent tales of time travel in either direction, no less than tales set
entirely in the future, force connections to real history presented
with some degree of cognitive estrangement rather than allowing as fantasies do the contemplation of worlds altogether dis-
connected from our own timestream.

In *A Connecticut Yankee*'s preface Mark Twain paradoxically
stresses both its close connection with history and its freedom
from the constraints of chronology by insisting that the "ungen-
tle" laws and customs mentioned in his story along with the

episodes illustrating them are historical although "it is not pretended that these laws and customs existed in England in the sixth century." Because they certainly existed later, Twain says, it is "no libel" to impute them to the sixth century, and anyhow "one is quite justified in inferring that wherever one of these laws or customs was lacking in that remote time, its place was competently filled by a worse one" (CY, "Preface." For Twain's sources, see the explanatory notes in CY, 455–75). Though Twain does not finally subscribe to any doctrine of unlimited progress, neither does he display nostalgia for the past. He draws on Arthurian lore as mediated by Malory's *Morte Darthur* to create an imaginary sixth century that although mythic is a receptacle for the anachronistic Yankee representing nineteenth-century American attitudes and technological capacities. It is also a receptacle for other anachronisms in the form of what Twain regarded on the basis of his reading in history books as actual laws and customs from later periods, most conspicuously ancien régime France and the antebellum American South, standing here for much of the cruelty, injustice, and fanaticism (as well as some of the absurdities) that stain all the pages of human history. Arthur's England, as experienced by the Connecticut Yankee and his readers, thus becomes a synecdoche for everything that is worst about the past: slavery; arbitrary imprisonment without trial; inequality before the law; rigid hierarchies in church and state that stifle intellectual as well as political freedom; absence of democracy; wanton unpunished killing of the defenseless by the powerful; exploitation of the poor by the rich; intolerance; superstition; ignorance; and sheer hardship of daily life for most people. Nor of course are these evils all safely confined to some remote past symbolized by the Yankee's sixth century, a point that Twain makes in various ways culminating in the final battle, which puts an end to Morgan's utopian schemes. The horrible past encountered by Twain's Connecticut Yankee is also an emblem of what still too often exists in our present, and of what despite technological and political progress may be humanity's bleak future.

Twain's indictment of human folly achieves great and in places truly Swiftian satiric power from such vividly narrated episodes as the visit to Morgan le Fay's castle and dungeons with their pitiful collection of unjustly imprisoned people who have wasted their lives chained in darkness; accounts of innocents burnt at the stake or (like Hank) almost burnt; the superstitious absurdities of the Valley of Holiness; Morgan and Arthur's visit to cottagers dying of smallpox while denied any help or comfort by their neighbors and clergy; and especially the callous mistreatment of slaves observed and then experienced by the Yankee and King Arthur (incidents modeled on accounts of slavery in the American South). What gives *A Connecticut Yankee* its distinctive force, however, is not merely Twain's very considerable narrative skill in presenting such episodes while modulating their tone back and forth from comedy through biting satire, pathos, and even tragedy. They also gain impact from his use of time travel to juxtapose fiction with reality. More precisely, he uses an intrusion of present (the Yankee) into past (Arthurian England) as a device for juxtaposing earlier with later modes of fictional narration, and fictional with factual modes of writing in order to suggest new ways of reading each in dialogue with the others.

For example, after describing the oppressions endured by freemen like those he and Sandy encounter "assembled in the early morning to work on their lord the bishop's road three days each—gratis," Morgan remarks that seeing this group "was like reading about France and the French, before the ever-memorable and blessed Revolution, which swept a thousand years of such villainy away in one swift tidal wave of blood" (CY, 111). For the Yankee his experience in Arthur's England is "like reading." It is like a history book brought to life. Our encounter with the freemen via his narrative *is* reading, but of a novel not history. Moreover, Twain implies that from this fictional moment resembling a history book we may learn how to interpret properly those history texts that present the French Revolution as centered on what to our eyes may (Twain fears) seem excessive use of the guillotine. Morgan, speaking here as so often for Twain, concludes from his encounter with the freemen that there were really

> two "Reigns of Terror," if we would but remember it and consider it: the one wrought murder in hot passion, the other in heartless cold blood, the one lasted mere months, the other had lasted a thousand years. . . . A city cemetery could contain the coffins filled by that brief

Terror which we have all been so diligently taught to shiver at and mourn over; but all France could hardly contain the coffins filled by that older and real Terror—that unspeakably bitter and awful Terror which none of us has been taught to see in its vastness or pity as it deserves. (CY, 111–12).

Here is one of Twain's eloquent passages of savage indignation whose effectiveness is enhanced by a temporal setting that allows us to grasp something of the past's true immensity in terms of social rather than impersonal geological time.

One purpose of A Connecticut Yankee's mythic sixth century filled with real horrors taken from many later periods is to readjust our emotional as well as intellectual response to accounts of the French Revolution by enlarging our temporal perspective on its events. And not just its events. Looking forward from the Yankee's curious vantage point earlier in time but outside real history is intended to widen every reader's temporal horizons, thereby allowing, Twain implies, a more accurate interpretation of any historical narrative dealing with one particular moment. Twain provides a lesson in reading history so that we may understand the urgency of revolution and its justification.

The most important dialogue in A Connecticut Yankee is between Twain's text and Malory's Morte Darthur. By weaving five extended quotations from what he first describes as "old Sir Thomas Malory's enchanting book" (CY, 2) into A Connecticut Yankee, Twain invites readers to weigh the claims of two styles, Malory's and his own, that stand for ancient and modern outlooks. Neither style alone, however, could produce Twain's new kind of story, which is more than the sum of its stylistic components and as much based on collaboration as on opposition between old and new ways of writing. Its emblem is the manuscript journal that "M.T." receives from Hank Morgan after they meet during their tour of Warwick Castle: "The first part of it— the great bulk of it—was parchment, and yellow with age . . . a palimpsest. Under the old dim writing of the Yankee historian appeared traces of a penmanship which was older and dimmer still—Latin words and sentences, fragments from old monkish legends" (CY, 7). A Connecticut Yankee too is a kind of palimpsest overwriting Malory, who in turn overwrote others, even as it gains animation from echoing what Twain calls the Mort

Darthur's "rich feast of prodigies and adventures . . . the fragrance of its obsolete names" that steep him "in a dream of the olden time" (CY, 2) as he sits at night by his fire at the Warwick Arms Inn after his tour of the Castle and reads Malory's chapter, reprinted on pages 2 and 3 of *A Connecticut Yankee*, telling "how Sir Launcelot slew two giants, and made a castle free." Malory's words become a prelude to the Yankee's account. They arouse expectations of something similar while inviting too the question of whether we really want a narrative that is exactly like Malory's.

A Connecticut Yankee's first chapter reveals the book's immediate formal origins. Whereas Mary Shelley had started *Frankenstein* after her dream of a grotesque scientific creation while trying to write a ghost story and winding up with something very different, Twain inaugurated the time travel tale after a dream of the past inspired by reading Malory led him to attempt a version of romance. Like Mary Shelley, Twain records an actual dream, although unlike her he does not mention it in his book:

> Dream of being a knight errant in armor in the middle ages. Have the notions and habits of thought of the present day mixed with the necessities of that. No pockets in the armor. No way to manage certain requirements of nature. Can't scratch. Cold in the head—can't blow—can't get at handkerchief, can't use iron sleeve. Iron gets red hot in the sun—leaks in the rain, gets white with frost and freezes me solid in winter. Suffer from lice and fleas. Make disagreeable clatter when I enter church. Can't dress or undress myself. Always getting struck by lightning. Fall down, can't get up.[20]

This dream, like the book to which it eventually gave rise, achieves its satiric rejection of past lifestyles—and writing styles—by what amounts to an amusing clash between romance conventions and those of the now more acceptable realistic novel with its emphasis on quotidian details.[21] Unburdened by the conventions of realism, Malory and his predecessors could present images of knights-errant in armor without pausing to consider any difficulties of actually wearing it, much less of wearing it for a long time. In *A Connecticut Yankee* as in the dream, Twain achieves comedy by retaining the heroic premise of romance—

adventures in the good old days of King Arthur—while intruding other styles as well as later attitudes.

Hank Morgan travels to a mythic past by way of being sent first into the pages of Malory's *Morte Darthur*. Episodes and passages from it, mostly without attribution, become part of what he experiences. Instead of reading Malory, he hears people speak words that we may recognize as coming from the *Morte Darthur*, and he is sometimes placed in the midst of episodes from its pages. But he has never read it. Twain invites us to notice his insertion into what becomes a kind of belated variant of Malory's text. But Morgan, no reader of the *Morte Darthur* or its predecessors, and indeed no reader of much beyond newspapers, neither recognizes nor comments on this aspect of his adventure. For him the leap is simply from present to past. For us it is from nineteenth-century fiction to a fifteenth-century romance that quickly becomes something else by virtue of Morgan's disruptive presence. Awareness of various relationships between *A Connecticut Yankee* and the *Morte Darthur*, of which Morgan is oblivious, compels readers to stand back and judge his actions from a vantage point outside the more limited framework of his own values and his own partial understanding of his whereabouts. Although Morgan is most often Twain's mouthpiece, it is finally necessary to distinguish between them in order to understand the complex meaning of *A Connecticut Yankee*. Malory's book is also Twain's device for getting there from here and taking readers with him. But just as later time travelers have to venture away from the machines that bring them to their destinations, so Twain sends his readers beyond the confines of the style that transports them to another era.

Soon after Morgan's arrival at Camelot he is charmed to hear, for the first time, Merlin narrate to the assembled courtiers of the Round Table—in words taken from the *Morte Darthur*, Book 1, chapter 25 but not identified as such by Morgan—how Arthur got his sword Excalibur from the Lady of the Lake. All the others at court, however (even the dogs), fall asleep because they have heard Merlin tell this tale again and again: "the droning voice droned on. . . . Some heads were bowed upon folded arms, some lay back, with open mouths that issued unconscious music; the flies buzzed and bit, unmolested, the rats swarmed softly out from a hundred holes, and pattered about, and made themselves at home everywhere; and one of them sat up like a squirrel on the king's head and held a bit of cheese in its hands and nibbled it, and dribbled the crumbs in the king's face with naive and impudent irreverence. It was a tranquil scene, and restful to the weary eye and the jaded spirit" (CY, 25–26). So much for Malory's ability to hold an audience after the novelty wears off. So much too for the romantic appeal of Arthur's court, the good old days, and those (like Tennyson) who view them with nostalgia. Morgan later quotes an article by of one of his fledgling newspaper reporters, actually an account of a tournament taken from the *Morte Darthur*. He commends its "antique wording" as "quaint and sweet and simple, and full of the fragrances and flavors of the time" but objects that it lacks the "whoop and crash and lurid description" of modern journalism (CY, 75). Although this criticism cuts both ways, it mainly serves to distance Malory's style from viable modern modes, including that of Morgan's narration and thus of *A Connecticut Yankee* as a whole. The more tedious older style becomes another symbol of outmoded attitudes.

During Hank's excursion of knight-errantry with Sandy she talks in the style of Malory, skillfully parodied by Twain, and also weaves into her conversation a long, rambling, seemingly pointless tale that we (but not she or Morgan) may recognize as taken verbatim from Book 4, chapters 16–18 of the *Morte Darthur*. When Morgan asks her a question in his (our) idiom about some knights in her tale, she requires a translation and then meditates on Hank's explanation that he wants to know where the knights live: "'Hang they out—hang they out—where hang—where do they hang out, ah, right so; where do they hang out. Of a truth the phrase hath a fair and winsome grace, and is prettily worded withal. I will repeat it anon and anon in mine idlesse, whereby I may peradventure learn it. Where do they hang out. Even so! already it falleth trippingly from my tongue; and forasmuch as—" (CY, 126–27). Less accepting, Hank unfairly but hilariously remarks, "If you've got a fault in the world, Sandy, it is that you are a shade too archaic" (CY, 130). Undaunted, she pushes on with her story, whose shapelessness moves Hank to observe in his journal that "she generally began without a preface, and finished without a result" (CY, 127). His major objection to her narration is that its "archaics are a little *too* simple; the vocabulary is too limited, and so, by consequence, descriptions suffer in the matter of variety; they run too much to level Saharas of fact, and not enough to picturesque detail. . . . the fights are all alike . . . just ghosts scuffling in a fog" (CY, 130–31). Twain's bill of complaint against what even for Malory's day was deliberately old-fashioned writing in the *Morte Darthur* becomes by inversion a prescription for properly telling and judging a tale: highest marks are given for vividness, variety, and brisk movement to an ending that makes a difference.

Toward the conclusion of *A Connecticut Yankee*, Malory's account of King Arthur's final battle with Sir Mordred is quoted (again without attribution) as another bit of reportage for one of Morgan's newspapers and praised by him as "a good piece of war correspondence" (CY, 417). The tragic denouement of Malory's *Morte Darthur*—whose conclusion, far from being without a result, suggests the gravest consequences of Arthur's last war—is thus juxtaposed with and incorporated into the parallel events that destroy the Yankee's utopian project. Here by including as a lauded part of *A Connecticut Yankee*'s exposition this last quote from Malory, Twain again narrows (without closing) the stylistic gap between his book and its fifteenth-century analogue. This reconvergence of styles is part of a larger movement in which the past reasserts itself against Morgan's attempt to displace it by introducing modern attitudes and artifacts.

Morgan's marriage to Sandy, and their child, symbolize in a positive way the past's inescapable claims. It is a marriage of convenience that becomes true love and (improbably) ideal companionship: "She was a flawless wife and mother; and yet I had married her for no particular reason, except that by the customs of chivalry she was my property until some knight should win her from me in the field. . . . Within the twelvemonth I became her worshiper; and ours was the dearest and perfectest comradeship that ever was" (CY, 406–7). Other aspects of the past intrude in less pleasant ways that doom the promise of this marriage between nineteenth- and sixth-century outlooks. After traveling to France with Sandy because their ailing child needs a better climate for a while, Hank is called back to England to find that all his efforts at progress have suddenly collapsed in the wake of Arthur's war with Mordred (as described in Malory and other Arthurian romances). Moreover (and this along with some bits about stock exchange manipulation helping to precipitate the civil war is Twain's addition to the romance versions of the Round Table's end), the Church has placed an interdict on the country to alienate its inhabitants from Morgan's modernizing efforts. Trains no longer run. Telegraphs and telephones no longer work. Electricity no longer illuminates Camelot: "the Church laid a ban upon the electric light!" (CY, 419). Twain stresses the symbolism of this renewed darkness: "From being the best electric-lighted town in the kingdom, and most like a recumbent sun of anything you ever saw, it was become simply a blot. . . . it made me feel as if maybe it was symbolical—a sort of sign that the Church was going to *keep* the upper hand, now, and snuff out all my beautiful civilization just like that" (CY, 410). With his only remaining followers, 52 boys educated under the Yankee's new Enlightenment regime and therefore unswayed by old prejudices or loyalties, Morgan retreats to Merlin's cave, where earlier he had secretly installed a large electrical generator while "projecting a miracle" in case another (technological) one should be necessary (CY, 420), and which he now fortifies for a last stand against the reactionary forces of chivalry and the Church.

That Morgan can find no more suitable refuge than the old magician's haunt remodeled with electric lights and modern weaponry is another ominous sign of human inability to break away from the past. So is the absence among Morgan's followers at this penultimate moment of any women who might help propagate a new society. Sandy and the child remain in France. There are only young soldiers doomed to perish along with Morgan's hopes for a better world. From Merlin's cave Morgan proclaims a republic, but it attracts no adherents among a population raised under the old regime. They are afraid to defy the interdict. Their incapacity for democracy and their subservience to the Church become Twain's final proof of Morgan's earlier observation (apropos Morgan le Fay's cruelty) that "training is everything; training is all there is to a person. We speak of nature; it is folly; there is no such thing as nature; what we call by that misleading name is merely heredity and training" (CY, 162). The irony of this assumption about the plasticity of human nature is that it is at once a warrant for optimistic Enlightenment belief like Morgan's that society can be newly modeled on some utopian plan if only everybody is properly educated or reeducated, and warrant too for pessimistic conviction that long-standing deplorable attitudes can never be replaced by better ones. It may be a less intentional irony of *A Connecticut Yankee*'s conclusion, which shows an incipient technological utopia destroyed, that Twain's ferociously anticlerical dramatization of how ancient superstitions mobilized by the Church overwhelm the modernizing champions of reason can be read as illustrating with equal clarity the inescapable presence of original sin.

The apocalyptic Battle of the Sand-Belt fought outside Merlin's cave is nineteenth-century science fiction's most disturbing image of industrialized warfare, inevitably read now as a grim forewarning of the horrors that were to unfold in the trenches of World War I and as a forewarning too of the even greater horrors possible after Hiroshima. Twain's intention was less prophecy than diagnosis of industrial civilization's darkest potentialities for self-destruction. That self-destruction, moreover, is also portrayed by him as peculiarly dehumanizing because advanced technology replaces individual encounters of warrior against warrior at close range with alienated forms of death that reach out at long distance and strike down people who never know exactly what or who has killed them.

Twain invites attention to this eerie feature of modern warfare—in turn emblematic of alienation in modern life—by including for purposes of contrast at the end of that last quotation from the *Morte Darthur* presented as "a good piece of war correspondence" Malory's gruesome—and remarkably vivid—account of Mordred and Arthur exchanging deathblows:

> Then the king gat his spear in both his hands, and ran toward Sir Mordred, crying, Traitor, now is thy death day come. And when Sir Mordred heard Sir Arthur, he ran until him with his sword drawn in his hand. And then king Arthur smote Sir Mordred under the shield, with a foin of his spear throughout the body more than a fathom. And when Sir Mordred felt that he had his death's wound, he thrust himself, with the might that he had, up to the bur of king Arthur's spear. And right so he smote his father Arthur with his sword holden in both his hands, on the side of the head, that the sword pierced the helmet and the brain-pan, and therewithal Sir Mordred fell stark dead to the earth. And the noble Arthur fell in a swoon to the earth, and there he swooned oft-times. (CY, 417)

This father and son locked in deadly close combat with one impaled on the other's spear are no pale ghosts scuffling in a fog. It is an unforgettable image. Twain's last reprise of Malory allows a glimpse of that master writer at his best, to underscore the even more horrific conditions of war after the industrial revolution had created a class of technicians like Twain's Yankee who (as he boasts early in the narrative) learned his trade at "the great Colt arms-factory . . . learned to make everything: guns, revolvers, cannon, boilers, engines, all sorts of labor-saving machinery" (CY, 4). As the Battle of the Sand-Belt unfolds Twain ironically invests the notion of labor-saving machinery (the foundation of technological utopias like Bellamy's *Looking Backward*) with a sinister new range of meaning.

For the Yankee's side at least, the side of industrialized society, combat need not involve anything like the face-to-face exertions of Arthur and Mordred. The first wave of massed chivalry attacking Merlin's cave—"Innumerable banners fluttering . . . horsemen—plumed knights in armor" (CY, 430)—hits a belt of dynamite land mines whose explosion creates a large ditch while blasting the knights into forms no longer recognizably human: "Of course we could not *count* the dead, because they did not exist as individuals, but merely as homogeneous protoplasm, with alloys of iron and buttons" (CY, 432). Such modern war may not even leave corpses, just an anonymous residue of organic and inorganic substance scrambled together.

Since Hiroshima, America's symbol of ultimate horror has been the image of one commander hidden away in some bunker pushing a button that unleashes Armageddon simultaneously from hundreds of bombers, missile silos, and warships that send weapons to destroy an enemy whose last act is to retaliate in kind. Fear of such mutually assured destruction (with its appropriate acronym MAD) has been taken by some theorists as in fact the major deterrent to an all-out atomic exchange. Whatever the validity of this theory, *A Connecticut Yankee*'s conclusion remarkably resonates with twentieth-century nightmares centering on that convenient labor-saving button by which a technologically advanced civilization commits suicide. Twain's push-button warfare extends from the battlefield to the cities as Morgan (after humanely warning people away) eliminates all the factories that he has built but also mined and equipped with underground wires leading to a detonator at his headquarters in Merlin's cave: "I touched a button and shook the bones of England loose from her spine! In that explosion all our noble civilization-factories went up in the air, and disappeared from the earth. It was a pity, but it was necessary. We could not afford to let the enemy turn our own weapons against us" (CY, 430–32). Only by destroying their advanced technology—and with it their advanced civilization—are its creators made safe from its abuse. The Yankee describes how electrified fences just outside Merlin's cave have—at the flick of a switch on his part—electrocuted most of the enemy who next attempt a night attack: "Our camp was enclosed with a solid wall of the dead—a bulwark, a breastwork, of corpses. . . . One terrible thing about this thing was the absence of human voices; there were no cheers, no war cries: being intent upon a surprise, these men moved as noiselessly as they could; and always when the front rank was near enough to their goal to make it proper for them to begin to get a shout ready, of course they struck the fatal line and went down without testifying" (CY, 439). Here not only the pageantry but the very sounds of war are replaced by a haunting silence as men die unseen and unseeing without even the satisfaction of confronting those whom they fight and articulating as Malory's Arthur can the reason why they fight.

Morgan reports that he touched yet another "button and set fifty electric suns aflame on the top of our precipice" (CY, 439). Their baleful artificial glare discloses the defenders "enclosed in three walls of dead men" while rendering the remaining attackers "paralyzed . . . petrified . . . with astonishment" (CY, 439). Before they can recover from their surprise at the appearance of Morgan's miniature suns (an ironic echo of his more welcome "miracle" in seeming to abolish the eclipse), he closes another switch that "shot the current through all the fences and struck the whole host dead in their tracks! *There* was a groan you could *hear!* It voiced the death-pang of eleven thousand men" (CY, 440). As for the rest, "The thirteen gatlings began to vomit death into the fated ten thousand," who mostly drown upon retreating to the encircling ditch (created by the initial explosion of land mines), into which Morgan's young soldiers at his signal divert water from a mountain brook, thus making a new "river a hundred feet wide and twenty-five deep" (CY, 440). Here is technology's landscape gardening of death.

The Yankee has won: "we fifty-four were masters of England! Twenty-five thousand men lay dead around us" (CY, 440). But the victory is also defeat, as Clarence observes, because it is impossible to remain healthy in the presence of so many decaying bodies breeding disease and stench: "We were in a trap, you see—a trap of our own making. If we stayed where we were, our dead would kill us; if we moved out of our defences, we should no longer be invincible" (CY, 443). Morgan is stabbed while trying to help one of the enemy's wounded—a romantic chivalrous gesture at odds with both the modern warfare he has introduced and the realities of medieval warfare that he has elsewhere noted but failed to understand, and another sign of the past's fatal attraction for the Yankee despite all his efforts to abolish its influence even while surrounded by it. Merlin then reappears in disguise and succeeds in weaving a spell that sends the Yankee back to his own period via thirteen centuries of enchanted sleep. Morgan's utopian efforts have culminated in push-button warfare that reestablishes the Dark Ages. In resorting to magic as a means of winding up the plot by returning Morgan to the nineteenth century in the most stylistically old-fashioned way possible, A Connecticut Yankee's narrative has reverted to one of the conventional devices of Arthurian romance, thus again making its style a mirror of its paradoxical message that the past for all its absurdity and dangers cannot be evaded but may have valuable aesthetic if not ideological uses.

Critics have deplored what is usually seen as Twain's inartistically abrupt shift from optimism to pessimism in A Connecticut Yankee's last section, while remarking too the inconsistencies of Morgan's character as he wavers between Yankee huckster and passionate advocate of democracy and scientific enlightenment.[22] Other contradictions abound, most notably between the Yankee's pretensions to technological know-how and the little that he actually accomplishes via technology before the final battle. As Boss, he proves remarkably ineffectual. He has no real grasp of the political situation around him, its potential for undoing all his efforts, or the actual consequences for those whose lot he attempts to improve. Twain does little to prepare readers to accept Sandy at the end as Morgan's ideal but forever-lost love after they first encounter her at such length as little more than an amusing object of satire, including some lamentably chauvinist strokes on Morgan's part, if not Twain's, aimed at what is presented as female, not just medieval, verbosity, gullibility, and illogic. The Catholic Church as antagonist is also sketched in outlines more suitable to caricature drawn by a village atheist than serious portrayal of the competing claims of reason and faith, democracy and hierarchy. Except for Arthur's genuinely touching moment of sublime courage in helping the cottagers stricken with smallpox, and his almost equally but more comically sublime inability to understand how most of those he governs actually live, none of the familiar characters from Arthurian romance comes to life. They remain more ghostly than their counterparts in the *Morte Darthur*, whose presentation Twain finds inadequate.

Another charge against *A Connecticut Yankee* is Justin Kaplan's assertion that it is "a book which, as far as it preaches anything, preaches irreverence, the guillotine, a reign of terror, and a kind of generalized despair" (Kaplan, 296). Darko Suvin properly situates Twain among science fiction's pioneers, but finds that because of contradictions between *A Connecticut Yankee*'s initial affirmation of "the progressive theory of history" and "Twain's increasing alienation from the effects of the industrial revolution" his "book was left without a moral and political core—which is fatal equally for satire and utopia" (Suvin, 196). Such disappointment will certainly await those expecting *A Connecticut Yankee* to provide the usual satisfactions of satires, utopias, sermons with uplifting preachments, or even realistic novels with consistent characterization and uniformity of style.

Bud Foote is closer to the mark in noting affinities to "the more deliberately contrived breaks in credibility" in Brechtian epic theater while placing *A Connecticut Yankee* less in relationship to prior forms than to all those later time travel stories of which it is the archetype (Foote, 133). *A Connecticut Yankee*'s dialogue with the *Morte Darthur* also creates self-reflexive invitations to consider not just plot events and ideas but the book we are reading in relation to other books. Almost as much as time travel, such literary self-consciousness has become a hallmark of science fiction. As a genre it often resorts to methods that invite not suspension of disbelief or total immersion in plot and ideas, but a mental stepping back to answer the aesthetic question put explicitly by Wells's Time Traveller: "Taking it as a story, what do you think of it?"

One of *A Connecticut Yankee*'s greatest strengths is its dynamic movement from utopian beginning to anti-utopian conclusion. Twain avoids the tedium of works that fall entirely into one or another category. I doubt books are necessarily better for remaining generically stable or having a coherent and positive political philosophy as, for example, *Looking Backward* does. To preach irreverence as a permanent attitude always relevant under any government is far from despair, and it may lead in the end to more intelligent political action than proposing some plausible theory. It will certainly go further to sustain that comic spirit which *A Connecticut Yankee* as a whole advocates as a solution to the existential problem, more pressing than any political issue, that human life is perhaps nothing more than what Morgan, and through him Twain, describes as "this plodding sad pilgrimage, this pathetic drift between the eternities" (*CY*, 162). His praise of the guillotine and France's revolutionary reign of terror are not calls to similar action but are intended for shock value as one means of keeping alive sensitivity to oppression and its remedy, insofar as there is a political remedy: removal of the oppressors. Despite its apparent volte-face at the end, *A Connecticut Yankee* retains an altogether sufficient moral and political core because of the way it centers on the values, surely related, of laughter and democracy.

The sheer fun of its earlier parts, to which analysis like mine can hardly do justice, but that every reader will experience, is not canceled out by the final turn toward tragedy. The wreck of Morgan's utopian dreams in the cataclysmic Battle of the Sand-Belt would be much less forceful, for all of Twain's prescient diagnosis of modern warfare, if it were not for our impression, created by the preceding chapters, that something of inestimable value has been lost when the Yankee's republic dies at birth. The absurdist pathos of Morgan's death as recounted in the "Final P.S. by M.T." also invites nostalgia for the laughter of earlier portions, whose comedy is recalled to mind by Twain's wry description of the Yankee's delirious dying words as an attempt at "getting up his last 'effect'" (*CY*, 447). Something like the complementarity principle of physics is at work because, just as in that theory light must be taken as both waves *and* particles although these seem mutually exclusive states, *A Connecticut Yankee*'s pessimistic ending coexists with its optimistic beginning rather than erasing it. Twain not only introduced time travel, which in itself is a major accomplishment indispensable to viable science fiction. He also used it to convey with great comic vigor and moral force the inescapable paradox of living in an age of science: reason allied with technology offers humanity's best hope, even though it may tragically prove a vain hope, of escaping the tyrannies spawned by ignorance; but technology also poses the threat of placing us permanently in a new dark age.

Notes

Chapter 1

1. Mary Shelley, *Frankenstein; or, The Modern Prometheus* (New York and Scarborough, Ontario: Signet Classics, New American Library, 1963), xiii; hereafter cited in text as *Frankenstein.* This conveniently available text reprints *Frankenstein*'s third edition, for which Mary Shelley provided her "Author's Introduction" and final revisions.

2. William Wordsworth, "Preface to the Second Edition of the *Lyrical Ballads*," in *Criticism: The Major Texts*, ed. Walter Jackson Bate (New York: Harcourt, Brace & Co., 1952), 342.

3. Félix Bodin, *Le Roman de l'avenir* (Paris, 1834), 15–32.

4. See Paul Alkon, "Deus Ex Machina in William Gibson's Cyberpunk Trilogy," in *Fiction 2000: Cyberpunk and the Future of Narrative*, ed. George Slusser and Tom Shippey (Athens: University of Georgia Press, 1992), 75–87.

5. H. G. Wells, "Preface to *The Scientific Romances*," in *H. G. Wells's Literary Criticism*, ed. Patrick Parrinder and Robert M. Philmus (Sussex: Harvester Press; Totowa, N.J.: Barnes & Noble Books, 1980), 240.

6. Robert H. Sherard, "Jules Verne Re-visited," in *The Jules Verne Companion*, ed. Peter Haining (New York: Baronet Publishing Company, 1979), 59–60.

7. N. Katherine Hayles, *Chaos Bound: Orderly Disorder in Contemporary Literature and Science* (Ithaca, N.Y., and London: Cornell University Press, 1990), 277; emphasis added.

8. See Fredric Jameson, *Postmodernism; or, The Cultural Logic of Late Capitalism* (Durham, N.C.: Duke University Press, 1992), 39–44.

9. Mark Rose, *Alien Encounters: Anatomy of Science Fiction* (Cambridge, Mass.: Harvard University Press, 1981), 5; hereafter cited in text.

10. Samuel R. Delany, *Starboard Wine: More Notes on the Language of Science Fiction* (Pleasantville, N.Y.: Dragon Press, 1984), 89.

11. Darko Suvin, *Metamorphoses of Science Fiction: On the Poetics and History of a Literary Genre* (New Haven, Conn.: Yale University Press, 1979), 8, emphasis deleted; hereafter cited in text.

12. Pierre Versins, *Encyclopédie de l'utopie, des voyages extraordinaires, et de la science fiction* (Lausanne: Editions L'Age d'Homme, 1972), 7–8: "La conjecture romanesque rationnelle, c'est un point de vue sur l'univers, y compris l'Homme, et non un genre, ni une forme."

13. See Jonathan Swift, *The Annotated Gulliver's Travels*, ed. Isaac Asimov (New York: Clarkson N. Potter, 1980), 144, 147, 154, 157, 158, 197.

14. H. G. Wells, *Anticipations of the Reaction of Mechanical and Scientific Progress upon Human Life and Thought* (London: Chapman & Hall, 1902), 70; hereafter cited in text as *Anticipations*.

15. Arthur B. Evans, "Vehicular Utopias of Jules Verne," paper presented at the Maison d'Ailleurs Utopia conference, Yverdon-les-Bains, Switzerland, 18–24 June 1991.

16. Sylvia K. Miller, letter to the author.

Chapter 2

1. Bernard Bergonzi, *The Early H. G. Wells: A Study of the Scientific Romances* (Manchester, England: Manchester University Press, 1961), 45.

2. Mary Shelley, *The Last Man*, ed. Hugh J. Luke, Jr. (Lincoln: University of Nebraska Press, 1965), 326.

3. Anthony Burgess, "Introduction," in Daniel Defoe, *A Journal of the Plague Year*, ed. Anthony Burgess and Christopher Bristow (Harmondsworth, England: Penguin Books, 1972), 19.

4. Norman Spinrad, *Science Fiction in the Real World* (Carbondale and Edwardsville: Southern Illinois University Press, 1990), 82.

5. Mary Shelley, *Frankenstein; or, The Modern Prometheus* (New York and Scarborough, Ontario: Signet Classics, New American Library, 1963), 15; hereafter cited in text as *F*.

6. For an especially clear statement on the secularity of *Frankenstein*'s world, see George Levine, "The Ambiguous Heritage of *Frankenstein*," in *The Endurance of Frankenstein: Essays on Mary Shelley's Novel*, ed. George Levine and U. C. Knoepflmacher (Berkeley: University of California Press, 1979; reprint, 1982), 6–7. For endorsement of this view and perceptive remarks on the affinities of *Frankenstein* with both *Robinson Crusoe* and science fiction, see Chris Baldick, *In Frankenstein's Shadow: Myth, Monstrosity, and Nineteenth-Century Writing* (Oxford, England: Clarendon Press, 1987; reprint, 1990), 42.

7. See Lee Sterrenburg, "Mary Shelley's Monster: Politics and Psyche in *Frankenstein*," in *The Endurance of Frankenstein: Essays on Mary Shelley's Novel*, ed. George Levine and U. C. Knoepflmacher (Berkeley: University of California Press, 1979; reprint, 1982), 143–71. See also Ronald Paulson, *Representations of Revolution (1789–1820)* (New Haven, Conn.: Yale University Press, 1983), 239–47.

8. For an introduction to psychological approaches to *Frankenstein*, see William Veeder, *Mary Shelley and Frankenstein: The Fate of Androgyny* (Chicago: University of Chicago Press, 1986).

9. Peter Dale Scott, "Vital Artifice: Mary, Percy, and the Psychopolitical Integrity of *Frankenstein*," in *The Endurance of Frankenstein: Essays on Mary Shelley's Novel*, ed. George Levine and U. C. Knoepflmacher (Berkeley: University of California Press, 1979; reprint, 1982), 189.

10. Mrs. Loudon [Jane Webb], *The Mummy! A Tale of the Twenty-Second Century*, 2d ed. (London: Frederick Warne & Co; New York: Scribner, Welford & Armstrong, 1872), 108.

11. Brian Stableford, *Scientific Romance in Britain 1890–1950* (London: Fourth Estate, 1985), 13.

12. H. G. Wells, "Fiction about the Future," in *H. G. Wells's Literary Criticism*, ed. Patrick Parrinder and Robert M. Philmus (Sussex: Harvester Press; Totowa, N.J.: Barnes & Noble Books, 1980), 247.

13. George Orwell, "Wells, Hitler and the World State," in George Orwell, *Dickens, Dali and Others* (San Diego, Calif.: Harcourt Brace Jovanovich, n.d.), 123, 121.

14. H. G. Wells, "Preface to the Scientific Romances," in *H. G. Wells's Literary Criticism*, ed. Patrick Parrinder and Robert M. Philmus (Sussex: Harvester Press; Totowa, N.J.: Barnes & Noble Books, 1980), 241–42.

15. H. G. Wells, "The Food of the Gods and How It Came to Earth," in *The Complete Science Fiction Treasury of H. G. Wells* (New York: Avenel Books, 1978), 584.

16. Darko Suvin, *Metamorphoses of Science Fiction: On the Poetics and History of a Literary Genre* (New Haven, Conn.: Yale University Press, 1979), 243, n. 23; 232–33.

17. Frank McConnell, *The Science Fiction of H. G. Wells* (Oxford, England: Oxford University Press, 1981), 92.

18. See Karl S. Guthke, *The Last Frontier: Imagining Other Worlds, from the Copernican Revolution to Modern Science Fiction*, trans. Helen Atkins (Ithaca, N.Y.: Cornell University Press, 1990).

19. H. G. Wells, "The War of the Worlds," in *The Complete Science Fiction Treasury of H. G. Wells* (New York: Avenel Books, 1978), 266, 349.

20. Among the most elegant variations on Wells's trope of the beach at world's end are Nevil Shute's *On the Beach* (1957), the conclusion of Walter M. Miller's *A Canticle for Leibowitz* (1960), and J. G. Ballard's short story "The Terminal Beach" (1964).

21. H. G. Wells, *The Time Machine* (Toronto and New York: Bantam Books, 1982), 86; hereafter cited in text as *TM*.

22. See Lars Gustafsson, "The Present as the Museum of the Future," in *Utopian Vision, Technological Innovation and Poetic Imagination*, ed. Klaus L. Berghahn and Reinhold Grimm (Heidelberg: Carl Winter Universitätsverlag: 1990), 105–10.

Chapter 3

1. Bernard Blanc, *Pourquoi j'ai tué Jules Verne* (Paris: Editions Stock, 1978).

2. Jean-Pierre Andrevon, *Retour à la terre* (1975; reprint, Paris: Editions Denoël, 1977), 12. *Retour à la terre 2* appeared in 1976 and *Retour à la terre 3* in 1977, both also edited by Andrevon and published by Editions Denoël.

3. Marc Angenot, "Science Fiction in France before Verne," *Science Fiction Studies* 5:1 (1978), 58–66; Marie-Hélène Huet, "Anticipating the Past: The Time Riddle in Science Fiction," in *Storm Warnings: Science Fiction Confronts the Future*, ed. George E. Slusser, Colin Greenland, and Eric S. Rabkin (Carbondale: Southern Illinois University Press, 1987), 34–42; and Arthur B. Evans, *Jules Verne Rediscovered: Didacticism and the Scientific Novel* (New York: Greenwood Press, 1988), 159–62; hereafter cited in text.

4. See discussion in Chapter 2 and note 12.

5. See Paul K. Alkon, *Origins of Futuristic Fiction* (Athens: University of Georgia Press, 1987), 3–44, 89–114.

6. See Paul Alkon, "The Paradox of Technology in Mercier's *L'An 2440*," in *Utopian Vision, Technological Innovation and Poetic Imagination*, ed. Klaus L. Berghahn and Reinhold Grimm (Heidelberg: Carl Winter Universitätsverlag, 1990), 43–62. On the difficult question of relationships between books and social change in eighteenth-century France, see Roger Chartier, *The Cultural Origins of the French Revolution*, trans. Lydia G. Cochrane (Durham, N.C.: Duke University Press, 1991), especially chap. 4, "Do Books Make Revolutions?"

7. See W. Warren Wagar, *Terminal Visions: The Literature of Last Things* (Bloomington: Indiana University Press, 1982).

8. Emile Souvestre, *Le Monde tel qu'il sera* (Paris: W. Coquebert, 1846), 321; my translation.

9. "Avertissement de l'editeur," prefixed to the 1866 edition of *Voyages et aventures du capitaine Hatteras*, quoted and translated in Evans 1988, 30.

10. Andrew Martin, *The Mask of the Prophet: The Extraordinary Fictions of Jules Verne* (Oxford, England: Clarendon Press, 1990), 99; hereafter cited in text.

11. Jules Verne, *The Complete Twenty Thousand Leagues under the Sea*, trans. Emanuel J. Mickel (Bloomington: Indiana University Press, 1991), 156; hereafter cited in text as *TTL*. This has a very helpful introduction and is the best translation into English of Verne's entire text, which has been badly cut and unevenly rendered in most previous English versions. All Verne's novels have suffered in this way, to the great detriment of his reputation outside France. Even some widely read French editions have omitted much of Verne's text, thereby distorting awareness of his artistry. A reliable and easily available French edition, to which I will refer when providing my own translation in a few places where Verne's turn of phrase is especially important, is Jules Verne, *Vingt mille lieues sous les mers*, ed. Simone Vierne (Paris: Garnier-Flammarion, 1977), hereafter cited in text as *VML*. For my approach to Verne, I am much indebted to Vierne's excellent introduction. Another important English version, reasonably reliable in its translation and indispensable for its introduction and notes, is *The Annotated Jules Verne: Twenty Thousand Leagues under the Sea*, ed. Walter James Miller (New York: New American Library, 1976). On the severe problems created by inadequate English translations, see, in addition to comments by Mickel and Miller in their editions, Evans 1988, xiii–xv.

12. Marie-Hélène Huet, *L'histoire des Voyages Extraordinaires: essai sur l'oeuvre de Jules Verne* (Paris: Minard, 1973), 59–64.

13. H. G. Wells, *The Time Machine* (Toronto and New York: Bantam Books, 1982), 109.

14. Jules Verne, *Autour de la lune* (Paris: Editions Gallimard, 1977), 111; hereafter cited in text as *ADLL*. My translation.

15. See Pascal Ducommun, "Alien Aliens," in *Aliens: The Anthropology of Science Fiction*, ed. George E. Slusser and Eric S. Rabkin (Carbondale: Southern Illinois University Press, 1987), 36–42.

16. Arthur B. Evans, "Science Fiction in France: A Brief History," *Science Fiction Studies* 16:3 (1989), 254–76.
17. Villiers de l'Isle-Adam, *Tomorrow's Eve*, trans. Robert Martin Adams (Urbana: University of Illinois Press, 1982), 3.
18. The best account to date of relationships between actual science and science fiction is Peter Nicholls, David Langford, and Brian Stableford, *The Science in Science Fiction* (New York: Alfred A. Knopf, 1983).
19. See Arthur B. Evans, "Science Fiction vs. Scientific Fiction in France: From Jules Verne to J.-H. Rosny Aîné," *Science Fiction Studies* 44, vol. 15, part 1 (1988), 1–11.
20. See Dominique Lacaze, "Lectures croisées de Jules Verne et de Robida," in *Jules Verne et les science humaines*, ed. François Raymond and Simone Vierne (Paris: Union Générale D'éditions, 1979), 76–100.
21. Albert Robida, *Le Vingtième siècle* (Geneva: Editions Slatkine, 1981).
22. Marc Angenot, "Albert Robida's Twentieth Century," *Science Fiction Studies* 10:2 (1983), 237.

Chapter 4

1. Edgar Allan Poe, "The Pit and the Pendulum," in *Tales of Edgar Allan Poe*, intro. Hervey Allen (New York: Random House, 1944), 541; hereafter cited in text as *Tales*.
2. Edgar Allan Poe, "Mellonta Tauta," in *The Science Fiction of Edgar Allan Poe*, ed. Harold Beaver (Harmondsworth, England: Penguin Books, 1976), 310–11; hereafter cited in text as *PSF*.
3. H. Bruce Franklin, *Future Perfect: American Science Fiction of the Nineteenth Century*, rev. ed. (Oxford, England: Oxford University Press, 1978), 102–3; hereafter cited in text as *FP*.
4. Kingsley Amis, *New Maps of Hell: A Survey of Science Fiction* (New York: Harcourt, Brace & Co., 1960), 33–34.
5. Darko Suvin, *Metamorphoses of Science Fiction: On the Poetics and History of a Literary Genre* (New Haven, Conn.: Yale University Press, 1979), 151; hereafter cited in text.

6. Brian W. Aldiss, *Billion Year Spree: The True History of Science Fiction* (1973; reprint, New York: Schocken Books, 1975), 52.

7. On late-twentieth-century market forces that shape science fiction, see Cristina Sedgewick, "The Fork in the Road: Can Science Fiction Survive in Postmodern, Megacorporate America?," *Science Fiction Studies* #53, vol. 18, part 1 (March 1991), 11–52.

8. David Ketterer, *New Worlds for Old: The Apocalyptic Imagination, Science Fiction, and American Literature* (Bloomington: Indiana University Press, 1974), 52, 57; hereafter cited in text.

9. Edward Bellamy, *Looking Backward 2000–1887*, ed. Cecelia Tichi (Harmondsworth, England: Penguin Books, 1986), 65–66; hereafter cited in text as *LB*.

10. William Morris, review of *Looking Backward* for the January 1889 issue of *The Commonweal*, quoted in William Morris, *News from Nowhere; or, An Epoch of Rest: Being Some Chapters from a Utopian Romance*, ed. James Redmond (London: Routledge & Kegan Paul, 1970), xxxvii.

11. See Herbert L. Sussman, *Victorians and the Machine: The Literary Response to Technology* (Cambridge, Mass.: Harvard University Press, 1968).

12. H. Bruce Franklin, *War Stars: The Superweapon and the American Imagination* (New York and Oxford, England: Oxford University Press, 1988), 67.

13. Howard P. Segal, "The Technological Utopians," in *Imagining Tomorrow: History, Technology, and the American Future*, ed. Joseph J. Corn (Cambridge, Mass.: The MIT Press, 1986), 122–23, 118. See also Howard P. Segal, *Technological Utopianism in American Culture* (Chicago: University of Chicago Press, 1985); and Leo Marx, *The Machine in the Garden: Technology and the Pastoral Ideal in America* (New York: Oxford University Press, 1964), especially chap. 4, "The Machine."

14. See Peter Ruppert, *Reader in a Strange Land: The Activity of Reading Literary Utopias* (Athens: University of Georgia Press, 1986).

15. Peter Fitting, "Utopian Effect/Utopian Pleasure," in *Styles of*

Creation: Aesthetic Technique and the Creation of Fictional Worlds, ed. George Slusser and Eric S. Rabkin (Athens: University of Georgia Press, 1992), 154.

16. Mark Twain, *A Connecticut Yankee in King Arthur's Court*, ed. Bernard L. Stein (Berkeley: University of California Press, 1983), 393; hereafter cited in text as *CY*.

17. See W. M. S. Russell, "Time in Folklore and Science Fiction," *Foundation: The Review of Science Fiction* 43 (Summer 1988), 5–24.

18. See Ian P. Watt, "Time and Family in the Gothic Novel: *The Castle of Otranto*," *Eighteenth-Century Life* 10, n.s., 3 (October 1986), 159–71.

19. Bud Foote, *The Connecticut Yankee in the Twentieth Century: Travel to the Past in Science Fiction* (New York: Greenwood Press, 1991), 93–94; hereafter cited in text.

20. Clemens's note, in Justin Kaplan, *Mr. Clemens and Mark Twain: A Biography* (1966; reprint, New York: Simon & Schuster Touchstone Book, 1983), 293; hereafter cited in text.

21. See Ian Watt, *The Rise of the Novel: Studies in Defoe, Richardson and Fielding* (Berkeley: University of California Press, 1957).

22. Especially good on the difficulties as well as the virtues and genesis of *A Connecticut Yankee* is Henry Nash Smith, *Mark Twain's Fable of Progress: Political and Economic Ideas in "A Connecticut Yankee"* (New Brunswick, N.J.: Rutgers University Press, 1962).

Bibliographic Essay

Reference Works

A pioneering and still unsurpassed source for study of early science fiction is Pierre Versins, *Encyclopédie de l'utopie, des voyages extraordinaires et de la science fiction* (Lausanne: Editions L'Age d'Homme, 1972; 2d ed., 1984). This magnificent and handsomely illustrated work, unfortunately not available in translation, is a solo achievement in the great French tradition of crusading Enlightenment encyclopedists. Versins illuminates many remote corners of his vast topic, much of whose bibliographic history he was the first to discover thanks to inspired detective work as a book collector. Versins also makes a persuasive case throughout his articles for the aesthetic and ethical significance of the related forms of science fiction, utopias, and imaginary voyages that he groups together as novelistic rational conjecture about humanity's place in the universe. To supplement my remarks in chapter 1 on his *Encyclopedia*'s theoretical orientation and role in establishing the House of Elsewhere at Yverdon, Switzerland, I should stress here that Versins's articles usually provide strongly expressed opinions as well as sound bibliographic guidance. This is no dull repository of statistics, although it is an almost inexhaustible mine of relevant facts. Those who consult this volume will find themselves instructed, entertained, and above all challenged to arrive at their own ideas, whether in agreement or disagreement with Versins, on a remarkably wide range of works and forms that led to what we now call science fiction.

A collaborative effort with accurate articles by 34 expert contributors is *The Science Fiction Encyclopedia*, ed. Peter Nicholls (New York: Doubleday & Co., 1979). This is strongest on twentieth-century science fiction to its publication date, but altogether trustworthy where it touches on earlier works. For even wider coverage of earlier as well as post-1979 material, see its indispensable successor, *The Encyclopedia of Science Fiction*, ed. John Clute and Peter Nicholls (New York: St. Martin's Press, 1993).

Focusing on material written in English or translated into English from *Frankenstein* to 1930 but with some attention to major precursors is Everett F. Bleiler, *Science-Fiction: The Early Years* (Kent, Ohio: Kent State University Press, 1990). This includes plot summaries of more than 3000 stories, with author, title, and motif indexes. For the most part Bleiler provides information about publication and story lines rather than intruding critical opinions, while nevertheless making sound judgments on the relevance of borderline works to science fiction. He is especially helpful in showing the role—and proliferation—of magazine stories. For American science fiction, see Thomas D. Clareson, *Science Fiction in America, 1870s–1930s: An Annotated Bibliography of Primary Sources* (Westport, Conn.: Greenwood Press, 1984) and its companion narrative, Thomas D. Clareson, *Some Kind of Paradise: The Emergence of American Science Fiction* (Westport, Conn.: Greenwood Press, 1985). Both reveal the abundance of American material, but the latter is hampered by Clareson's uncertainty as to "whether 'science fiction' is so narrow and distinct, either in content or in form, that it makes up a separate and distinct genre" (*Some Kind of Paradise*, xiii). A useful bibliography on a more restricted topic, stories set in future time, is I. F. Clarke, *Tale of the Future from the Beginning to the Present Day*, 3d ed. (London: The Library Association, 1978). This has a chronological list starting in 1644, and also an author and short-title index. See too "Anticipation" in the Versins encyclopedia. For alternative histories, see Barton C. Hacker and Gordon B. Chamberlain, "Pasts That Might Have Been, II: A Revised Bibliography of Alternate History," in *Alternative Histories: Eleven Stories of the World As It Might Have Been*, ed. Charles G. Waugh and Martin H. Greenberg (New York: Garland, 1986), 301–63. This has informative brief annotations and is preceded (281–300) by Gordon B. Chamberlain's essay "Allohistory in Science Fiction."

Invaluable for those interested in all phases of science fiction is Neil Barron, *Anatomy of Wonder: A Critical Guide to Science Fiction*, 3d ed. (New York: R. R. Bowker Co., 1987). It has essays on the history of science fiction with annotated bibliographies of important works; essays on foreign-language science fiction (covering German, French, Russian, Japanese, Italian, Danish, Swedish, Norwegian, Dutch, Belgian, Romanian, Slovenian, Serbo-Croat or Croato-Serbian, Hungarian, Macedonian, and Hebrew); and chapters on various research aids including libraries and private collections. A fourth edition scheduled for publication under the same title will probably not include the essays on foreign-language science fiction and will therefore not altogether supplant the third edition, which should be consulted together with its successor volume.

The major Anglophone journals are *Science-Fiction Studies*, *Extrapolation*, and *Foundation: The Review of Science Fiction*. All provide attention to the history of science fiction, although its early days have received the most discussion, from many theoretical viewpoints, in *Science-Fiction Studies*, which also prints the most book reviews. *Imagine: science-fiction et littératures de l'imaginaire* is a lively French journal from Québec with fiction as well as criticism.

Historical and Theoretical Studies

For a genre as new and various as science fiction, historical surveys have had to be no less concerned with defining than outlining their subject. The most influential effort to date, thanks to its persuasively argued case for science fiction as the literature of cognitive estrangement, is Darko Suvin, *Metamorphoses of Science Fiction: On the Poetics and History of a Literary Genre* (New Haven, Conn.: Yale University Press, 1979). In addition to a definition that allows significant affiliation of science fiction to related forms as well as attention to its method of influencing readers and its relationship to social contexts (especially during the crucial nineteenth century), its greatest strength is Suvin's unequivocal insistence that science fiction at its best inseparably combines aesthetic, ethical, and cognitive dimensions. A corollary difficulty of Suvin's approach is that his application of ideological criteria, usually Marxist, to assess ethical soundness often overshadows analysis of aesthetic and cognitive strands in the works he singles out. Nor does he always pause for detailed explication of the texts whose ideologies he evaluates and locates with respect to changing social attitudes. But whatever is lost by Suvin's tilt toward ideological aspects of science fiction is more than compensated by the general soundness of his aesthetic judgments, the impressive historical scope of his survey, and the incisive way he challenges readers to take their own stand for or against his opinions. *Metamorphoses of Science Fiction* is the best introduction to the genre's theoretical issues, a book to be read first by way of preface to further study and then returned to frequently while encountering for oneself the texts it considers.

There are shrewd though brief observations on Verne and Wells from a novelist's perspective in Kingsley Amis, *New Maps of Hell: A Survey of Science Fiction* (New York: Harcourt, Brace & Co., 1960). This book presents the substance of lectures delivered at Princeton University's 1958–59 Christian Gauss Seminar in Criticism, an important first step toward appropriate academic attention to science fiction. More extensive chapters on early science fiction from Mary Shelley's precursors through H. G. Wells and his contemporaries occupy almost one half of Brian W. Aldiss, *Billion Year Spree: The True History of Science Fiction* (London: Weidenfeld & Nicolson, 1973). This lively study shows how the beginnings of science fiction looked to one of its best practitioners in the latter part of the twentieth century. Regrettably for those like myself who prefer Aldiss unadulterated, some of his most vivid and provocative statements in the first part of *Billion Year Spree* are watered down to achieve the more cautiously drab committee-prose of its jointly authored sequel, Brian Aldiss with David Wingrove, *Trillion Year Spree: The History of Science Fiction* (London: Victor Gollancz Ltd., 1986). This carries the history further into the twentieth century, where the proliferation of science fiction texts makes impractical a comprehensive single-handed survey by an active novelist who wishes to remain active. Since both Aldiss and Wingrove assume responsibility, however, it is never possible to tell exactly which opinions are those of Aldiss alone. I recommend searching out *Billion Year*

Spree both for its superior vigor and its greater value as evidence of how science fiction's early texts impressed a twentieth-century master of the form.

Another pioneering work (the first from a university press) very much worth consulting for its sophisticated view of science fiction as myth and rhetorical strategy is Robert M. Philmus, *Into the Unknown: The Evolution of Science Fiction from Francis Godwin to H. G. Wells* (1970; reprint, Berkeley: University of California Press, 1983). A good selection of early illustrations accompanies the first two chapters of David Kyle, *A Pictorial History of Science Fiction* (1976; reprint, London: Tiger Books International, 1986). The impact of science fiction on modern and postmodern visual imagination is most apparent in cinema, to which the best introduction is Vivian Sobchack, *Screening Space: The American Science Fiction Film*, 2d ed., enl. (New York: Ungar, 1988). Sobchack offers excellent commentary on key films, including the 1931 James Whale version of *Frankenstein* starring Boris Karloff, with illustrations well chosen to demonstrate the evolution of Hollywood's iconology of science fiction. In a perceptive discussion of affinities between science, magic, and religion as socially related methods of trying to control the unknown, Sobchack explains the puzzling ways in which films often combine the logically but not emotionally incompatible modes of science fiction and horror. In a chapter on "Postfuturism," Sobchack analyzes aesthetic implications of the recent collapse of temporal distinctions that threatens to annihilate the genre of science fiction by abolishing one of its major claims to differentiation from other forms: "If 'science fiction' was once a generic category predicated on speculating and imagining a probable or possible future, the genre seems endangered—its work now producing regressive fantasies on the one hand, and 'delirious' comedies totally absorbed in the material present on the other. Today's SF either nostalgically locates the future in an imagined past and thus articulates it as 'over,' or it complacently locates the future in the present, celebrating it as 'here,' and 'now'" (*Screening Space*, 300). It remains to be seen whether this trend will indeed spell the end of science fiction as a distinct genre in and outside film, as Sobchack fears. In any event, her persuasive analysis of this worrisome development—which is undoubtedly part of a larger and more sinister turn away from rational modes of apprehending our future and from confidence in facing it—certainly under-scores by contrast the significance of the early futuristic fiction that so strongly shaped the emergence of science fiction.

Among more specialized studies, incurable partiality and the importance of its topic impel me to mention first Paul K. Alkon, *Origins of Futuristic Fiction* (Athens: University of Georgia Press, 1987). Here I examine closely the first wave of stories set in future time with particular attention to key French contributions center-ing on emergence of alternative history, futuristic utopias, and the remarkably accurate poetics for futuristic fiction propounded in 1834 by Félix Bodin in his *Le Roman de l'avenir*. A study concerned more with attitudes toward the future than with the aesthetics of giving those attitudes literary shape is I. F. Clarke, *The Pattern of Expectation 1644–2001* (New York: Basic Books, 1979). For a survey of future wars, see I. F. Clarke, *Voices Prophesying War, 1763–1984* (London: Oxford University Press, 1966) and its second edition featuring extended though spotty coverage of more recent future wars and a "Checklist of Imaginary Wars, 1763–1990": I. F. Clarke, *Voices Prophesying War: Future Wars 1763–3749*, 2d ed. (Oxford, England: Oxford University Press, 1992).

The classic introduction to moon voyages through Verne remains Marjorie Hope Nicolson, *Voyages to the Moon* (1948; reprint, New York: Macmillan, 1960). Related matters are taken up from the viewpoint of intellectual rather than literary history, although in ways indispensable to understanding the context of early science fiction, in Karl S. Guthke, *The Last Frontier: Imagining Other Worlds from the Copernican Revolution to Modern Science Fiction*, trans. Helen Atkins (Ithaca, N.Y.: Cornell University Press, 1990; first published as *Der Mythos der Neuzeit*, Bern, Switzerland: A. Francke AG Verlag, 1983). Complementing this is Michael J. Crowe, *The Extraterrestrial Life Debate 1750–1900: The Idea of a Plurality of Worlds from Kant to Lowell* (Cambridge, England: Cambridge University Press, 1986). For important nine-teenth-century intellectual contexts taken up without reference to science fiction but nevertheless helpfully to its students, the best introduction remains Loren Eiseley, *Darwin's Century: Evolution and the Men who Discovered it* (Garden City, N.Y.: Doubleday & Co., 1958).

The case for a specifically British tradition stemming largely but not exclusively from what H. G. Wells called "scientific romance" is usefully made in Brian Stableford, *Scientific Romance in Britain 1890–1950* (London: Fourth Estate, 1985). British social contexts are examined in Darko Suvin, *Victorian Science Fiction in the UK: The Discourses of Knowledge and of Power* (Boston: G. K. Hall & Co., 1983). In addition to an essay on the social role of science fiction in Victorian England, Suvin includes an extensive bibliography of science fiction books published in the United Kingdom from 1848 to 1900 along with an essay on defining the boundaries of the genre and a valuable "Annotated Check-list of Books Not to Be Regarded as SF, with an Introductory Essay on the Reasonable Reasons Thereof." There are also biographical sketches of science fiction writers of the period, a social classification of them, and a brief but very informative essay by John Sutherland on nineteenth-century science fiction and the book trade. For other perspectives on the boundaries of science fiction viewed from outside, see Kathryn Hume, *Fantasy and Mimesis: Responses to Reality in Western Literature* (New York: Methuen, 1984). Also helpful in distinguishing the scope of fantasy is Eric S. Rabkin, *The Fantastic in Literature* (Princeton, N.J.: Princeton University Press, 1976). On utopias, see Peter Ruppert, *Reader in a Strange Land: The Activity of Reading Literary Utopias* (Athens: University of Georgia Press, 1986).

On French science fiction, see Arthur B. Evans, "Science Fiction in France: A Brief History," *Science Fiction Studies* #49, vol. 16, part 3 (November 1989): 254–76; and Arthur B. Evans, "Science Fiction in France: A Selective Bibliography of Secondary Materials," *Science Fiction Studies* #49, vol. 16, part 3 (November 1989): 338–68.

Anthologies

For excellent interpretive essays amounting to a lucid history of its topic, as well as for a fine selection of major stories, see H. Bruce Franklin, *Future Perfect: American Science Fiction of the Nineteenth Century*, rev. ed. (London: Oxford University Press, 1978). G. T. Chesney's "The Battle of Dorking" is included with other works and a fascinating introduction by Michael Moorcock in *Before Armageddon: An Anthology of Victorian and Edwardian Fiction Published before 1914*, Vol. 1, ed. Michael Moorcock (1975; reprint, London: Wyndham Publications, Star Book, 1976).

Related stories are available in *Science Fiction by Gaslight: A History and Anthology of Science Fiction in the Popular Magazines, 1891–1911*, ed. Sam Moskowitz (Cleveland and New York: World, 1968). Some very scarce texts, including most notably Albert Robida's droll "Jadis chez aujourd'hui," are provided (with concise commentary) in *La Science-fiction avant la SF: Anthologie de l'imaginaire scientifique français du romantisme à la pataphysique*, ed. Monique Lebailly (Paris: Editions de L'Instant, 1989).

Individual Writers and Works

The vitality of Mary Shelley's *Frankenstein* is attested by a proliferation of discussions that shows no sign of abating. To appreciate the range of its appeal for our time in and outside the borders of science fiction, start with *The Endurance of Frankenstein: Essays on Mary Shelley's Novel*, ed. George Levine and U. C. Knoepflmacher (Berkeley: University of California Press, 1979). A notable feminist reading is provided in "Horror's Twin: Mary Shelley's Monstrous Eve," Chapter 7 of Sandra M. Gilbert and Susan Gubar, *The Madwoman in the Attic: The Woman Writer and the Nineteenth-Century Literary Imagination* (New Haven, Conn.: Yale University Press, 1979), 213–47. Other feminist and psychological issues are dealt with in William Veeder, *Mary Shelley & Frankenstein: The Fate of Androgyny* (Chicago: University of Chicago Press, 1986) and Mary Lowe-Evans, *Frankenstein: Mary Shelley's Wedding Guest* (New York: Twayne, 1993). Monstrosity as image, trope, and myth from *Frankenstein* forward, with nice remarks on H. G. Wells among others, is the topic of Chris Baldick, *In Frankenstein's Shadow: Myth, Monstrosity, and Nineteenth-Century Writing* (Oxford, England: Clarendon Press, 1987). Earlier attitudes toward monstrosity, especially in relationship to ideas about the feminine role in procreation, provide the context for an important discussion of *Frankenstein*'s genesis in Marie-Hélène Huet, *Monstrous Imagination* (Cambridge, Mass.: Harvard University Press, 1993). A survey (from the perspective of deconstructive criticism) of how textual complications in *Frankenstein* shape readers' responses is provided in Fred Botting, *Making Monstrous: Frankenstein, Criticism, Theory* (Manchester, England: Manchester University Press; New York:

St. Martin's Press, 1991). Of fictions paying homage to Mary
Shelley's novel the best—and the best antidote to an overdose of
criticism—is Brian Aldiss, *Frankenstein Unbound* (London:
Jonathan Cape, 1973), a tale of time travel from twenty-first-century America to the villa by Lake Geneva where Mary Shelley is
writing *Frankenstein*.

To pursue H. G. Wells the best starting point is Frank
McConnell, *The Science Fiction of H. G. Wells* (Oxford, England:
Oxford University Press, 1981). Themes, dialectical structures,
and rhetorical strategies in Wells's fiction are lucidly analyzed in
John Huntington, *The Logic of Fantasy: H. G. Wells and Science
Fiction* (New York: Columbia University Press, 1982). The *fin de
siècle* context is explained in Bernard Bergonzi, *The Early H. G.
Wells: A Study of the Scientific Romances* (Manchester, England:
Manchester University Press, 1961). For important essays on
Wells, see *H. G. Wells and Modern Science Fiction*, ed. Darko Suvin
with Robert M. Philmus (Lewisburg, Pa.: Bucknell University
Press; London: Associated University Presses, 1977); *H. G. Wells
Under Revision: Proceedings of the International H. G. Wells
Symposium, London, July 1986*, ed. Patrick Parrinder and
Christopher Rolfe (Selinsgrove, Pa.: Susquehanna University
Press; London: Associated University Presses, 1990); and *Critical
Essays on H. G. Wells*, ed. John Huntington (Boston: G. K. Hall &
Co., 1991). Two recent editions include illuminating commentary
and relevant material by Wells: *The Definitive Time Machine: A
Critical Edition of H. G. Wells's Scientific Romance with Introduction
and Notes*, ed. Harry M. Geduld (Bloomington: Indiana
University Press, 1987); and H. G. Wells, *The Island of Doctor
Moreau: A Variorum Text*, ed. Robert M. Philmus (Athens:
University of Georgia Press, 1993).

For Jules Verne the outstanding study to date in English is
Arthur B. Evans, *Jules Verne Rediscovered: Didacticism and the
Scientific Novel* (New York: Greenwood Press, 1988). This necessary book clears away many misconceptions, especially those
caused by poor translations largely responsible for the notion
that Verne should be dismissed as no more than a writer for children. Evans invites appreciation of Verne's complex artistry
while making a useful case too for distinguishing his science fiction from later modes because "his portrayed universe is highly
mimetic and in close alignment with the ideological mandates of

his times . . . the hermeneutic structure of his texts is patterned on various time-honored literary topoi and very traditional modes of referentiality" and because he engages in "overtly explicit and nonconjectural didacticism" (Evans, 160). Evans also traces significant continuities, especially in the social role of science fiction as a cultural shock absorber for dealing with rapid change. Another revisionist study making the case (more familiar in France) for Verne as a sophisticated writer and especially stressing his complex interrogation as well as affirmation of mainstream ideologies is Andrew Martin, *The Mask of the Prophet: The Extraordinary Fictions of Jules Verne* (Oxford, England: Clarendon Press, 1990). Less subtle but nevertheless worthwhile for a rapid overview is Peter Costello, *Jules Verne: Inventor of Science Fiction* (New York: Charles Scribner's Sons, 1978). Also useful as a basic introduction is Lawrence Lynch, *Jules Verne* (New York: Twayne, 1992). Very helpful commentary is provided in *The Annotated Jules Verne: Twenty Thousand Leagues under the Sea*, ed. Walter James Miller (New York: New American Library, 1976); and in *The Annotated Jules Verne: From the Earth to the Moon*, ed. Walter James Miller (New York: Thomas Y. Crowell, 1978). Interesting essays and illustrations are brought together in Peter Haining, *The Jules Verne Companion* (New York: Baronet, 1979). In *Jules Verne Rediscovered*, Evans includes an excellent and extensive bibliography of primary and secondary sources. This may be supplemented by Jean-Michel Margot, *Bibliographie documentaire sur Jules Verne* (Amiens, France: Centre de Documentation Jules Verne, 1989).

The continuing relevance of Villiers de l'Isle-Adam's *Tomorrow's Eve* is attested by Raymond Bellour, "Ideal Hadaly," in *Close Encounters: Film, Feminism, and Science Fiction*, ed. Constance Penley, Elisabeth Lyon, Lynn Spigel, and Janet Bergstrom (Minneapolis: University of Minnesota Press, 1991), 107–30. The book-length study that Albert Robida deserves remains to be written in some utopian future that I hope will be near rather than far. Meanwhile I can only refer you back to my discussion in chapter 3 and the references in its notes 20 and 22, along with the articles (mentioned in the foregoing) by Evans on French science fiction.

Mark Twain's too often overlooked or denigrated contributions to science fiction are briefly but accurately noted by

H. Bruce Franklin in *Future Perfect*, and located more precisely with respect to Twain's successors in Bud Foote, *The Connecticut Yankee in the Twentieth Century: Travel to the Past in Science Fiction* (New York: Greenwood Press, 1991). See too for a perceptive discussion of *A Connecticut Yankee*'s contexts David Ketterer, *New Worlds for Old: The Apocalyptic Imagination, Science Fiction, and American Literature* (Bloomington: Indiana University Press, 1974).

Ketterer also considers Poe's fiction and Bellamy's *Looking Backward* in the context of American apocalyptic visions. For commentary on Bellamy in our time as well as a bibliography of major studies, see *Looking Backward 1988–1888: Essays on Edward Bellamy*, ed. Daphne Patai (Amherst: University of Massachusetts Press, 1988). Intellectual and social contexts of *Looking Backward* and related technological utopias are explored in Howard P. Segal, *Technological Utopianism in American Culture* (Chicago: University of Chicago Press, 1985). On Edgar Allan Poe, see the bibliography and commentary in *The Science Fiction of Edgar Allan Poe*, ed. Harold Beaver (Harmondsworth, England: Penguin Books, 1976).

The works I have mentioned all provide notes or bibliographies that lead to other readings, of which the journals also provide an abundance. The golden age of science fiction studies is now. Even this rapid tour of beginning places for additional investigation shows that the best science fiction before 1900 retains its power to challenge and fascinate. The large number of university press books on this topic shows that visions most often regarded as marginal before Hiroshima are now widely acknowledged as central to the concerns of our time. Certainly too our intense scrutiny of early works has been motivated by desire to understand twentieth-century science fiction, and by recognition of it as a form very much in dialogue with its past. This speaks well for a genre whose readers have taken to heart Orwell's warning that loss of cultural memory is a fatal step on the pathway to dystopia.

Recommended Titles

A select list including some works published shortly after 1900

Abbott, Edwin A. (1838–1926), writing as "A Square." *Flatland: A Romance of Many Dimensions*. London: Seeley & Co., 1884. Social and religious satire via a story told by an inhabitant of a two-dimensional world (Flatland) who describes the social hierarchies and psychological foibles of his country while also narrating his adventures traveling to one- and three-dimensional space. He tells too the cautionary tale of a three-dimensional spherical visitor who causes trouble by trying to enlighten Flatlanders about aspects of the universe that they cannot perceive. This witty mathematical fantasy is a classic in the line of Swiftian games with perspective that have strongly influenced science fiction's preoccupation with social issues approached through rigorous though not necessarily plausible "thought experiments."

Bellamy, Edward (1850–1898). *Looking Backward, 2000–1887*. Boston: Ticknor, 1888. The most famous and influential American utopia. See discussion in text.

Bodin, Félix (1795–1837). *Le Roman de l'avenir* (The novel of the future). Paris: Félix Locquin, 1834. Scarce and not yet translated, this incomplete futuristic novel is notable for a remarkable preface that sets forth a viable poetics of futuristic fiction as a manifesto to encourage the development of that form. Bodin was the first to articulate an aesthetics for science fiction.

Bulwer-Lytton, Edward George Earle (1803–1873). *The Coming Race*. London: Blackwood, 1871. H. G. Wells, Edward Bellamy, and others were much influenced by this ideologically confused dystopian tale of an underground civilization filled with scientific marvels maintained by a mysterious energy source (called *vril*) and organized socially according to conventions that are partly attractive but ultimately menacing to the narrator, who tells of his subterranean encounter, narrow escape, and fear that when the underground people someday emerge they will take over the world. *The Coming Race* reflects ambiguous Victorian attitudes toward women and science.

Burroughs, Edgar Rice (1875–1950). *A Princess of Mars*. Chicago: McClurg, 1917. First published as by "Norman Bean" in *All-Story* magazine, February–July 1912. From the inventor of Tarzan, an immensely popular (and undeniably engaging) tale of high adventures on Mars, notable as an archetype for varieties of space opera and "Sword and Sorcery" fantasy too often confused with science fiction.

Butler, Samuel (1835–1902). *Erewhon; or, Over the Range*. London: Truebner, 1872. A satiric dystopia on the margins of science fiction, most notable for its parodic adaptation of Darwinian ideas to depict a society that has abandoned machinery out of fear that machines would otherwise evolve to displace humans.

Chesney, Sir George Tomkyns (1830–1895). *The Battle of Dorking*. Anon., first in *Blackwood's Magazine*, then separately, London: Blackwood, 1871. This initiated the future-war tale. See discussion in text.

Cyrano de Bergerac, Savinien (1619–1655). *Histoire comique des états et empires de la lune* (*Comic History of the States and Empires of the Moon*; Paris: Le Bret, 1657); and *Histoire comique des états et empires du soleil* (*Comic History of the States and Empires of the Sun*; Paris: Charles de Sercy, 1662). These first posthumous editions, the former from a manuscript to which Cyrano gave the title *L'Autre monde ou les états et empires de la lune* (The other world, or the states and empires of the moon), were expurgated by Henry le Bret to avoid offending the Church. There have been various English translations since the seventeenth century, of which the standard is *Other Worlds: The Comic History of the States and Empires of the Moon and the Sun*, trans. Geoffrey Strachan (New York: Oxford University Press, 1965). This fantasy of travel to countries of the moon and sun is usually accepted within the boundaries of science fiction or at least its precursors by virtue of off-planet settings used for purposes of cognitive estrangement, and because of Cyrano's daring social satire centering on concern with then-controversial issues of natural philosophy. It is the best as well as the most beautiful of the early moon voyages, influential for the development of that form, and also an important archetype for the Swiftian and Voltarian philosophical tale of travel and ideas.

Defontenay, Charlemagne-Ischir (1819–1856). *Star ou Psi de Cassiopée: Histoire merveilleuse de l'un des mondes de l'espace*. Paris: Le Doyen, 1854; reprint, Paris, Editions Denoël, 1972. *Star (Psi Cassiopeia)* by

C.-I. Defontenay, trans. P. J. Sokolowski, intr. Pierre Versins, illustrations by George Barr. New York: Daw Books, 1975. An extraordinarily inventive but not influential depiction of a complex alien culture, including samples of its literature and history, set in an intricate planetary system illuminated by three stars radiating light of different colors.

Doyle, Sir Arthur Conan (1859–1930). *The Lost World*. London: Hodder and Stoughton, 1912. From the inventor of Sherlock Holmes, the first Professor Challenger story: of an expedition to a remote plateau in South America where dinosaurs, pterodactyls, and pithecanthropi still survive. A classic of dealing with the past by importing it into the present.

————. *The Poison Belt: Being an Account of Another Amazing Adventure of Professor Challenger*. London: Hodder and Stoughton, 1913. Here the earth passes through a region of poisonous gas that temporarily immobilizes the planet's population except for Challenger and a few other scientific witnesses who have provided themselves with a supply of oxygen. A minor classic in the genre of catastrophes from outer space.

Flammarion, Nicolas Camille (1842–1925). *La Fin du monde*. Paris: Flammarion, 1893. Trans. as *Omega: The Last Days of the World*. New York: Cosmopolitan, 1894. An oddly appealing mixture of satire, utopia, scientific forecast, philosophical dissertation, popularized astronomy, history of beliefs about the world's end, and spiritualist preachments dramatized in a final episode when the spirit of the Pharaoh Cheops arrives during the last day to take the souls of the protagonists Omegarus and Eva to Jupiter, the next destination for human evolution in our solar system. In translation this variation on Grainville's *Last Man* was more influential for Anglophone writers of sweeping cosmological fantasies in the vein of Olaf Stapledon's *Last and First Men* (1930) and *Star Maker* (1937).

Forster, E(dward) M(organ) (1879–1970). "The Machine Stops." First published in the *Oxford and Cambridge Review*, Michaelmas Term, 1909. Written in opposition to the world state advocated in *A Modern Utopia* (1905) by H. G. Wells, this famous story depicts a future of ant-heap underground cities controlled by vast machinery that finally breaks down, thus liberating humanity to try again with less dependence on machines.

Gilman, Charlotte Perkins (1860–1935). *Herland*. First published without much impact in Gilman's magazine *The Forerunner* (January–December 1915), this vision of a utopia populated entirely by females has found its audience in the more profeminist milieu of the late twentieth century after publication in book form (London: Women's Press Limited, 1979; New York: Pantheon Books, 1979). Written almost a century after *Frankenstein, Herland's* current vogue signals the tenuous but significant thread of continuity linking early science fiction with its present renaissance as a genre ideally suited to exploration of gender issues.

Geoffroy-Château, Louis-Napoléon (1803–1858). *Napoléon et la conquête du monde—1812 à 1832—histoire de la monarchie universelle* (Napoleon and the conquest of the world—1812 to 1832—history of the universal monarchy). Published anonymously, Paris: Delloye, 1836. The second edition was published as by Louis Geoffroy with the title by which it is best known: *Napoléon apocryphe: histoire de la conquête du monde et de la monarchie universelle, 1812–1832* (The apocryphal Napoleon: History of the conquest of the world and of the universal monarchy, 1812–1832; Paris: Paulin, 1841). As yet untranslated, the most accessible edition is a reprint issued by Editions Tallandier (Paris, 1983). See discussion in text. This is the first book-length alternative history, brilliantly inaugurating the mode whose twentieth-century classic is Philip K. Dick's *The Man in the High Castle* (1962).

Grainville, Jean-Baptiste Xavier Cousin de (1746–1805). *Le Dernier homme* (*The Last Man*; Paris: Deterville, 1805). Most widely read in a second edition with a preface by Charles Nodier: *Le Dernier homme, ouvrage posthume* (Paris: Febra et Deterville, 1811). Translated anonymously as *The Last Man; or, Omegarus and Syderia, A Romance in Futurity* (London: R. Dutton, 1806). This tale of a future plague that wipes out humanity inaugurated the secular mode of stories recounting the end of human history.

Haggard, Sir Henry Rider (1856–1925). *She: A History of Adventure.* London: Longmans, Green, 1887. This tale of reincarnation and trekking through Africa to find the cruel, almost-immortal Ayesha, She-Who-Must-Be-Obeyed, though impossible to put down and fascinating for what it reveals (most often unintentionally) about Victorian attitudes toward sexuality and females, is a classic example of fantasy, not science fiction. It is utterly and irritatingly devoid of invitations to consider any aspect of the human situation rationally. Paradoxically, however, the quasi-realism of archaeological details in *She* (along with Haggard's other lost-world stories, especially *King Solomon's Mines*, 1885, and *Allan Quatermain*, 1887), has strongly influenced the treatment within science fiction of related themes of uncanny discoveries in remote, exotic places on our planet.

Kepler, Johannes (1571–1630). *Somnium.* Frankfurt, 1634. The definitive English edition is *Kepler's Somnium: The Dream, or Posthumous Work on Lunar Astronomy*, trans. with commentary by Edward Rosen. Madison: University of Wisconsin Press, 1967. Astronomical observations and speculations in a tale of travel to the moon made this a classic of proto–science fiction, although it is now of more historical than literary interest because its speculative (and real) science overshadows the fiction.

Lasswitz, Kurd (1848–1910). *Auf zwei Planeten.* Leipzig: Verlag B. Elischer

Nachfolger, 1897. Available in English only in an abridgement that severely cuts the text: *Two Planets: Auf zwei Planeten, a novel by Kurd Lasswitz*, abridged by Erich Lasswitz, trans. Hans H. Rudnick, afterword by Mark R. Hillegas. Carbondale and Edwardsville: Southern Illinois University Press, 1971. Published just before H. G. Wells's *The War of the Worlds* (1898), Lasswitz's story imagines an ultimately more benign invasion from Mars that results in establishment of a kind of rational utopia after an interval of warfare and partial domination of earth by the more technologically advanced Martians. Like Wells, Lasswitz makes a tale of invaders from outer space into an allegory of relationships between colonized and colonizers, but he does so with more attention to social rather than military and power relationships. *The War of the Worlds* achieves greater symbolic force through its concision and focus. *Two Planets* had less direct impact on Anglophone and French science fiction but strongly influenced German science fiction and, even more important, the imagination of German scientists such as Wernher von Braun, who contributed to the development of rockets that extended the reach of warfare and led also to space travel. *Two Planets* and *The War of the Worlds* provided the most significant paradigms for twentieth-century science fiction dealing with alien encounters as speculation or allegory.

London, Jack (1876–1916). *The Iron Heel*. New York: Macmillan, 1907. This futuristic dystopia telling of how a capitalist oligarchy establishes a totalitarian system in the United States is an important forerunner of Orwell's *Nineteen Eighty-Four*, written with passion and some persuasiveness in its analysis of American social problems, but with insufficient novelistic action to sustain interest through all of its preachments. For shorter works, see *The Science Fiction of Jack London: An Anthology*, ed. Richard G. Powers, Boston: Gregg Press, 1975.

Mercier, Louis-Sébastien (1740–1814). *L'An deux mille quatre cent quarante: rêve s'il en fut jamais* (The year 2440: A dream if ever there was one). Amsterdam: Van Harrevelt, 1771. There is no recent translation. William Hooper's 1795 version, which unaccountably rounds off the title to *Memoirs of the Year Two Thousand Five Hundred* and makes a few other small changes, was made available in a Gregg Press reprint (Boston: 1977). The best French edition, with an excellent introduction and Mercier's original text (which he later revised to take into account the achievement of balloon flight by the Montgolfier brothers in 1783), is *L'An deux mille quatre cent quarante: rêve s'il en fut jamais*, ed. Raymond Trousson (Bordeaux: Editions Ducros, 1971). *L'An 2440*, with its vision of a better Paris in the twenty-fifth century, inaugurated the crucial shift of utopia from the imaginary island to future time. See discussion in text.

Morris, William (1834–1896). *News from Nowhere; or, An Epoch of Rest*.

Being Some Chapters from a Utopian Romance. London: Reeves and Turner, 1891. First published in *Commonweal*, 11 January–4 October 1890. As the most famous response to Edward Bellamy's *Looking Backward* (1888), *News from Nowhere* is notable as a counterutopia proposing a more pastoral, less mechanized future based on Morris's idealized vision of the fourteenth century. Fortunately, science fiction writers have been little influenced by its cloying sentimentality, Luddite attitudes, and lack of narrative interest.

Poe, Edgar Allan (1809–1849). See discussion in text. His most important stories with an affinity to science fiction are "The Unparalleled Adventure of One Hans Pfaall" (1835); "The Balloon Hoax" (1844); "Mesmeric Revelation" (1844); and "Mellonta Tauta" (1849). These and others are collected with a useful introduction in *The Science Fiction of Edgar Allan Poe*, ed. Harold Beaver (Harmondsworth: Penguin Books, 1976).

Robida, Albert (1848–1926). Illustrator and writer who established the first complete iconography of the future. See discussion in text. His most important works, none yet translated into English or available in reprint editions except for an excellent facsimile of *Le Vingtième siècle* (Geneva: Editions Slatkine, 1981), are *Le Vingtième siècle* (The twentieth century; Paris: Dentu, 1883); *La Vie électrique* (The electric life; Paris: La Libraire illustrée, 1883); and *La Guerre au vingtième siècle* (War in the twentieth century; Paris: 1887).

Rosny Aîné, J. H. (pseudonym of Joseph-Henri Honoré Boëx, 1865–1940). "Les Xipéhuz" (Paris: Savine, 1887 in collection, and 1888 separately) imagines truly alien aliens along with a prehistoric setting in a short story that has strongly influenced French science fiction, although remaining comparatively unknown among Anglophone readers and writers. See discussion in text. *La Mort de la terre* (*The Death of the Earth*; Paris: Plon-Nourrit, 1910) is a far-future tale of humanity's extinction. Both are available in *The Xipehuz and the Death of the Earth*, trans. George E. Slusser (New York: Arno Press, 1978). Recent French editions are *La Force mystérieuse suivi de les Xipéhuz* (Paris: Nouvelles Editions Oswald, 1982); and *La Mort de la terre* (Paris: Editions Denoël, 1983). ·

Serviss, Garrett Putnam (1851–1929). *Edison's Conquest of Mars.* First published in the *New York Evening Journal*, 12 January–10 February 1898. Reprint, Los Angeles: Carcosa House, 1947 with intro. and bibliography by A. Langley Searles. This unauthorized sequel to H. G. Wells's *The War of the Worlds* (1898) is a classic example of bad science fiction in the mode of space opera appealing to those with a taste for jingoistic, xenophobic fantasy centering on myths of the scientist as newfangled magician and better weapons as the world's salvation.

Shelley, Mary Wollstonecraft (1797–1851). *Frankenstein; or, The Modern Prometheus.* London: Lackington, Hughes, Harding, Mavor, and Jones, 1818, published anonymously. Third edition, revised, published as by Mary Shelley with the addition of an author's introduction, London: Colburn, 1831. The beginning of modern science fiction. See discussion in text.

———. *The Last Man*. Published as by "the author of Frankenstein," London: Colburn, 1826. Less seminal than *Frankenstein* and more liable to limited biographical interpretation, but nevertheless a noteworthy experiment in the literature of futuristic catastrophe. See comments in text.

Souvestre, Emile (1805–1854). *Le Monde tel qu'il sera* (The world as it will be). Paris: W. Coquebert, 1846. This brilliantly illustrated and very funny satiric warning against the dangers of mechanization inaugurates the mode of futuristic dystopia perfected by George Orwell in the more grim tones of *Nineteen Eighty-Four*. See discussion in text.

Stevenson, Robert Louis (1854–1894). *The Strange Case of Dr. Jekyll and Mr. Hyde*. London: Longmans, Green, 1886.

Twain, Mark (pseudonym of Samuel Langhorne Clemens, 1835–1910). *A Connecticut Yankee in King Arthur's Court*. Illustrations by Daniel Carter Beard. New York: Charles L. Webster, 1889. Published also in England as *A Yankee at the Court of King Arthur* (London: Chatto and Windus, 1889). The archetypal story of travel to and from the past. See discussion in text.

Verne, Jules (1828–1905). See discussion in text. Here only the most significant of his works in or on the borders of science fiction are listed, along with a few reliable translations. Verne's reputation has notoriously suffered from incomplete or otherwise inadequate translations. Where none is mentioned, exercise caution or, better, your French.

———. *Cinq semaines en ballon* (*Five Weeks in a Balloon*). Paris: Hetzel, 1863. Verne's debut in the genre of extraordinary voyages that he turned in the direction of science fiction.

———. *Voyage au centre de la terre*. Paris: Hetzel, 1864. *Journey to the Center of the Earth*. Trans. Robert Baldick. New York: Penguin, 1965.

———. *De la terre à la lune*. Paris: Hetzel, 1865. *The Annotated Jules Verne: From the Earth to the Moon*. Trans. Walter James Miller. New York: Crowell, 1978.

———. *Vingt mille lieues sous les mers*. Hetzel, 1870. Verne's most important as well as most famous work: the place to embark on his extraordinary voyages for those wishing to understand their contribution to science fiction. *The Complete Twenty Thousand Leagues under the Sea*. Trans. Emanuel J. Mickel. Bloomington: Indiana University Press (Visions Series, Harry M. Geduld, General Editor), 1991. Another helpful edition is *The Annotated Jules Verne: Twenty Thousand Leagues under the Sea*. Trans. Walter James Miller. New York: New American Library, 1977.

———. *Autour de la lune* (*Around the Moon*). Paris: Hetzel, 1870.

————. *Le Tour du monde en quatre-vingts jours*. Paris: Hetzel, 1873. *Around the World in Eighty Days*. Trans. Jacqueline and Robert Baldick. New York: E. P. Dutton, 1968. An international best-seller that encouraged the growing taste in fiction and in life for speed and mobility.

————. *L'Ile mystérieuse* (*The Mysterious Island*). Paris: Hetzel, 1874–75. A Robinsonade that includes a reprise of Captain Nemo.

————. *Hector Servadac*. Paris: Hetzel, 1877. In this Robinsonade a passing comet takes into space a big chunk of earth along with a few people who must cope with their predicament and figure out how to return.

————. *Les Cinq Cents Millions de la Bégum* (*The 500 Millions of the Bégum*; translated also as *The Bégum's Fortune*). Paris: Hetzel, 1879. Verne's dystopian portrait of the regimented German weapons-manufacturing city of Stahlstadt (Steel City) is a warning against totalitarianism as well as against potential misapplication of modern science to warfare.

————. *Robur le conquérant* (Robur the conqueror; trans. as *The Clipper of the Clouds*). Paris: Hetzel, 1886. Verne here presents flight as an ambiguous symbol of the future.

————. *Sans dessus dessous* (*The Purchase of the North Pole*). Paris: Hetzel, 1889. A sequel to *From the Earth to the Moon* and *Around the Moon*, involving an attempt by the Baltimore Gun Club, which fortunately fails, to change the axis of the earth.

————. *Maître du monde* (*The Master of the World*). Paris: Hetzel, 1904. As in *The Purchase of the North Pole*, Verne's increasing pessimism about science is articulated in this tale of Robur's further adventures attempting to dominate the world with his flying machine, which is eventually destroyed by lightning along with its power-mad inventor.

Villiers de l'Isle-Adam, Jean-Marie-Mathias-Philippe-Auguste de (1838–1889). *L'Eve future*. Paris: M. de Brunhoff, 1886. *Tomorrow's Eve*. Trans. Robert Martin Adams. Urbana: University of Illinois Press, 1982. Issues of identity and gender are explored in this tale of an artificial woman created by the American inventor Edison. See discussion in text.

Webb, Jane (1807–1858). *The Mummy: A Tale of the Twenty-Second Century*. London: Henry Colburn, 1827. In this tale of the Pharaoh Cheops revived in a distant future whose details are very fully worked out, Webb satirizes nineteenth-century attitudes while also taking a big step toward solving the problem of how to incorporate interesting novelistic action within the static framework of a futuristic utopia or dystopia. See discussion in text.

Wells, Herbert George (1866–1946). See discussion in text. Listed here are his most significant early contributions to science fiction.

————. *The Time Machine*. London: Heinemann, 1895.

———. *The Stolen Bacillus and Other Incidents*. London: Methuen, 1895. Short stories.

———. *The Island of Doctor Moreau: A Possibility*. London: Heinemann, 1896.

———. *The Plattner Story and Others*. London: Methuen, 1897. Short stories.

———. *The Invisible Man: A Grotesque Romance*. London: Pearsons, 1897.

———. *The War of the Worlds*. London: Heinemann, 1898.

———. *When the Sleeper Wakes: A Story of Years To Come*. London and New York: Harper, 1899.

———. *Tales of Space and Time*. London: Harper, 1899.

———. *The First Men in the Moon*. London: Newnes, 1901.

———. *The Food of the Gods, and How It Came to Earth*. London: Macmillan, 1904.

———. *A Modern Utopia*. London: Chapman & Hall, 1905.

———. *In the Days of the Comet*. London: Macmillan, 1906.

———. *The War in the Air and Particularly How Mr. Bert Smallways Fared While It Lasted*. London: George Bell and Sons, 1908.

———. *The Country of the Blind and Other Stories*. London: Thomas Nelson, 1911.

———. *The World Set Free: A Story of Mankind*. London: Macmillan, 1914.

INDEX

INDEX

Caxton, William, 117
Cazotte, Jacques, 61
Chamisso, Adalbert von: *Peter Schelmihls wundersame Geschichte*, 44
Chesney, Sir George T.: *The Battle of Dorking*, 39–40; *The New Ordeal*, 40.
Civil War (American), 112
Clarke, Arthur C., 6
Clement, Hal: *Mission of Gravity*, 3
Cognitive estrangement, 10–11, 34, 67
Coleridge, Samuel Taylor: *The Rime of the Ancient Mariner*, 32
Columbus, Christopher, 17
Comedy, 137
Cyborgs, 8
Cyrano de Bergerac, Savinien, 57; *Comic History*, 18, 23

Darwin, Charles Robert, 20, 50, 51; *On the Origin of Species by Means of Natural Selection*, 19
Darwin, Erasmus, 4, 5
Defoe, Daniel: *Consolidator*, 24; *Journal of the Plague Year*, 24, 25, 62; *Robinson Crusoe*, 17, 23–24, 25, 27, 34–35, 62, 106, 119–20
Defamiliarization, 10–11, 34, 67
Democracy, 105, 116, 137
Delany, Samuel R., 10, 11
Descartes, René, 56, 82
Dial (magazine), 105
Dick, Philip K., 26, 114
Dickens, Charles, 109
Diderot, Denis, 56
Disneyland, 98
Doyle, Arthur Conan, 58

Edison, Thomas Alva, 84–88, 108
Emerson, Ralph Waldo, 101, 105
Enterprise: name of real and imaginary spaceships, 9
Epics, 2, 3
Epistolary novel, 26
Evans, Arthur B., 18, 67, 71
Evolution, 19, 20, 50, 51

Fantasy, 6, 25, 30, 39, 107, 113, 120, 121–23
Faust legend, 29–30, 32–33
Feminist themes, 37–38, 84–89, 98
Fitting, Peter, 114
Foote, Bud, 120, 121, 123, 136
Franco-Prussian War, 67–68
Franklin, Benjamin, 101
Franklin, Bruce, 105, 106
French Revolution, 33, 61–62, 125–26
Fulton, Robert, 9
Futuristic fiction, 21, 58–64

Garnett, David, *Lady into Fox*, 44
Galileo, 11
Genre: combinations of in particular works, 100, 137; determinants of, 11; retrospective identification of, 10; stability of, 137; *See also* epics, epistolary novel; futuristic fiction; Gothic fiction; historical novels; imaginary voyages; psychological novel; Robinsonade; science fiction, definitions of; short story; and utopias
Geoffroy-Château, Louis: *Napoléon et la conquête du monde*, 64–65, 119
Gernsback, Hugo, 8, 105
Ghost stories, 2; *see also* Gothic fiction
Gibson, William, 102; *Count Zero*, 6; *Mona Lisa Overdrive*, 6; *Neuromancer*, 6, 18
Godwin, Francis: *Man in the Moone*, 23
Godwin, Mary Wollstonecraft, *A Vindication of the Rights of Women*, 37
Godwin, William, 37
Goethe, Johann Wolfgang von: *The Sorrows of Young Werther*, 34, 35
Gothic fiction, 2, 25, 39, 102, 104, 118
Grainville, Jean-Baptiste Cousin de: *Le dernier homme*, 62
Grandville (pseud. of Jean-Ignace-Isidore Gérard), 89

Pascal, Blaise, 82, 83; *Pensées*, 19–20
Plato: *Republic*, 10
Poe, Edgar Allan, 8, 23, 102–107, 114;
"The Balloon Hoax," 102; "The
Cask of Amontillado," 102; "The
Conversation of Eiros and
Charmion," 104; "A Descent
into the Maelström," 80, 104;
"Eureka," 104; "The Facts in the
Case of M. Valdemar," 104;
"Mellonta Tauta," 103–104;
"Mesmeric Revelation," 104; *The
Narrative of A. Gordon Pym*, 78,
79; "The Pit and the
Pendulum," 102; "Some Words
with a Mummy," 104–105; "A
Tale of the Ragged Mountains,"
104; "The Unparalleled
Adventure of One Hans Pfaall,"
103
Pohl, Frederik: *Gateway*, 26
Point of view, 5–6, 7, 22–23, 26–27,
31, 34, 39, 45–46, 48
Prediction, 28, 43, 49, 71, 79, 100
Polidori, John, 4
Progress, 50, 51, 103, 104–105
Psychological novel, 25–26, 57, 74–75,
114–115; *see also* Villiers de
l'Isle-Adam, *Tomorrow's Eve*

Radcliffe, Anne, 4
Rashomon (film), 26
The Reign of George VI 1900-1925
(anon.), 40
Restif de la Bretonne, Nicolas-Edme:
Les Posthumes, 61–62
Richardson, Samuel: *Clarissa*, 26
Rip Van Winkle, 113
Robida, Albert, 89–100; *Les Aventures
très extraordinaires de Saturnin
Farandoul*, 90; *La Guerre au XXᵉ
siecle*, 90; *L'Horloge des siècles*, 90;
L'Ingénieur von Satanas, 90; *Jadis
chez aujourd'hui*, 90; *La Vie élec-
trique*, 90; *Le Vingtième siècle*,
90–100; *Voyage de fiançailles au
XXᵉ siècle*, 90
Robinsonade, 17, 99, 106, 120

Robots, 84–89, 97
The Rocky Horror Picture Show (film),
26
Romance, 127–28
Romanticism, 26, 69, 73
Roosevelt, Theodore, 102
Rose, Mark, 10
Rosny, J.-H. Aîné (pseudonym of
Joseph-Henri Honoré Boëx): *La
Mort de la terre*, 84; *Les
Navigateurs de l'infini*, 84; *The
Xipehuz*, 83–84
Russen, David: *Iter Lunare*, 23

Sartre, Jean-Paul, 53
Science, 4–6, 7, 11, 13, 15, 29–30,
44–45, 47, 49, 71–72, 79, 80–82,
84–85, 88
Science fiction: and astronomy,
19–20; boundaries of, 107; contexts and precursors of, 15–21;
definitions and aesthetics of,
1–15; emotion and reason in,
2–3; extensions of outside literature, 8–9; feminist themes in,
37–38, 84–89, 98–99; and future
settings, 20–21; and geology, 20;
iconography of, 90–97; and literature of exploration, 17–18;
and microscope, 19–20; and
mythology of science, 84–85;
and myths, 7; origins of term, 8;
and psychology, 25–26, 57, 86;
and publishing methods, 40–41;
and religion, 19; and romanticism, 26, 69, 73; self-referentiality in, 38, 54, 89–90, 136; and
short story, 106; and telescope,
19–20; temporal settings of, 25;
and time concepts, 20, 100; and
urbanization, 18–19; and
verisimilitude, 5, 88, 121–23; *See
also* fantasy; futuristic fiction;
Gothic fiction; history; illustrations; prediction; psychological
novel; science; time travel
Scott, Peter Dale, 37
Scott, Ridley: *Blade Runner*, 3, 18

About the Author

Paul Alkon is Leo S. Bing Professor of English at the University of Southern California. He has also taught at Berkeley, Maryland, Minnesota, and Ben Gurion University of the Negev. In the 1983–84 academic year he held a Guggenheim Fellowship. He has served as Book Review Editor for *Eighteenth-Century Studies* and on the editorial boards of *Eighteenth-Century Studies*, *The Age of Johnson*, and *The Eighteenth Century: Theory and Interpretation*. In 1989 he was elected President of the American Society for Eighteenth-Century Studies. Among his publications are *Samuel Johnson and Moral Discipline* (1967), *Defoe and Fictional Time* (1979), and *Origins of Futuristic Fiction* (1987) as well as essays on eighteenth-century topics, on Gertrude Stein, and on William Gibson. In 1989 his *Origins of Futuristic Fiction* won the Eaton Award for best critical work on science fiction of its year.

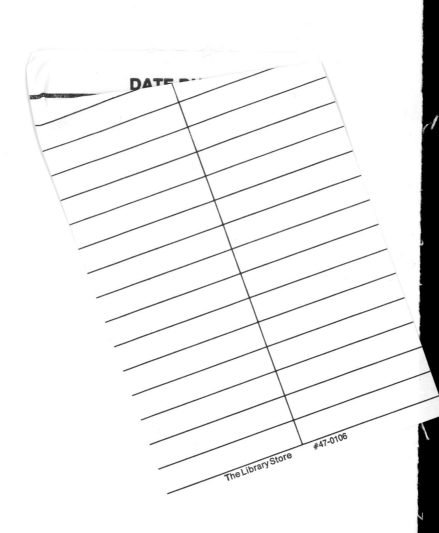